Everyman, I will go with thee,
and be thy guide

THE EVERYMAN
LIBRARY

The Everyman Library was founded by J. M. Dent
in 1906. He chose the name Everyman because he wanted
to make available the best books ever written in every
field to the greatest number of people at the cheapest possible
price. He began with Boswell's 'Life of Johnson';
his one-thousandth title was Aristotle's 'Metaphysics',
by which time sales exceeded forty million.

Today Everyman paperbacks remain true to
J. M. Dent's aims and high standards, with a wide range
of titles at affordable prices in editions which address
the needs of today's readers. Each new text is reset to give
a clear, elegant page and to incorporate the latest thinking
and scholarship. Each book carries the pilgrim logo,
the character in 'Everyman', a medieval mystery play,
a proud link between Everyman
past and present.

LEGENDS OF
ALEXANDER THE GREAT

Translated and Edited by
RICHARD STONEMAN

EVERYMAN
J. M. DENT · LONDON
CHARLES E. TUTTLE
VERMONT

Text, introduction and endmatter
© J. M. Dent, 1994

This edition first published in Everyman in 1994

J. M. Dent
Orion Publishing Group
Orion House, 5 Upper St Martin's Lane,
London WC2 9EA
and
Charles E. Tuttle Co. Inc.
28 South Main Street,
Rutland, Vermont 05701, USA

Typeset in Sabon by CentraCet Limited, Cambridge
Printed in Great Britain by
The Guernsey Press Co. Ltd, Guernsey, C.I.

British Library Cataloguing-in-Publication Data
is available upon request.

ISBN 0 460 87514 0

CONTENTS

NOTE ON THE EDITOR

RICHARD STONEMAN is an editor and writer specialising in Greek history and literature. He has translated the Greek *Alexander Romance* and is co-editor (with John Morgan) of a volume of essays entitled *Greek Fiction*. His other books include works on Greek antiquities, the *Traveller's History of Turkey* and *Palmyra and its Empire*.

For Christina

INTRODUCTION

I ALEXANDER THE GREAT: A MEDIEVAL HERO

The storie of Alisaundre is so commune
That every wight that hath discrecioun
Hath herd somwhat or al of his fortune

wrote Geoffrey Chaucer in *the Monk's Tale*.[1] Alexander the
Great (356–23 BC), the military genius who had brought much
of the known world under the rule of Greek-speaking Macedonians, was indeed a household name in the European Middle
Ages, where he had taken on the characteristics not just of a
conqueror, but of a perfect knight, a discoverer and inventor; he
had battled with fabulous beasts and strange races of men,
exchanged philosophical argument with Indian sages, and visited the Earthly Paradise. His name was often cited as a moral
exemplar for kingship, liberality, wisdom and closeness to God,
as well as for arrogant, covetous ambition. Parallel but different
developments took place contemporaneously, or earlier, in the
Jewish and Muslim worlds.

Alexander was even thought to have a special connection with
Britain. As early as the fourteenth century the French Romance
Perceforest had sought to link the story of Alexander with the
Arthurian legends of Britain. According to this work, Alexander's ship was swept off course soon after his conquest of
India, and blown ashore in Britain, where he made his lieutenants Betis and Gadifer kings of England and Scotland respec-
tively. Alexander was thus established – if uneasily – in the
legendary past of Britain, as a distant ancestor of Arthur, and
particularly in Scotland, whose kings, several of them named
Alexander, liked to trace their pedigree to the conqueror.[2]

The stories about his life and adventures were widely known, and texts proliferated. The French *Roman d'Alexandre*,[3] composed in the twelfth century, influenced the English and German traditions beginning from the early thirteenth century.[4] In both of these Alexander is seen as a hero of medieval chivalry: his campaigns are usually described as being directed against the Saracens, and long passages are devoted to descriptions of battles on horseback, to the colourful tents on the battlefield, and to the romantic relations (*Minne*, Courtly Love) pertaining between the knights and their ladies at home.[5] This medieval Alexander is, it need hardly be said, a far cry from the world conqueror of the fourth century BC. The metamorphosis from Macedonian warrior king to courtly hero is a touchstone of European sensibility over sixteen centuries, and because of the great number of texts about him this development can be studied in action at numerous points throughout that period. The texts collected in this book are representative of the least known of these late antique and early medieval traditions.

There were four main channels of transmission of stories about Alexander from antiquity to the authors of the medieval texts.

The first, which Chaucer follows in the account of Alexander's career (to which the above lines are the introduction), is the historical one as given by Quintus Curtius Rufus,[6] a writer of the first or second century AD, whose history, though not the most reliable, is perhaps the most readable and entertaining of the ancient histories. Quintus Curtius was the source for the epic poem in Latin by Walter of Chatillon (1178) which was probably Chaucer's inspiration for his references.[7] Some episodes of this are referred to also by John Gower in his *Confessio Amantis*.[8]

Secondly, there was the Alexander Romance.[9] This Greek work, which may have been composed as early as the third or second century BC, went through numerous Greek recensions in antiquity and was translated twice into Latin, first by Julius Valerius before 338 AD and secondly by Leo the Archpriest of Naples in the tenth century. Leo's work is lost but was the basis of a longer version of Alexander's adventures in Latin, known as the *Historia de Proeliis*, of which there exist three recensions, each expanding on the last.[10] Chaucer was certainly acquainted with this work also, since in the *House of Fame*[11] he refers to the story of Alexander's ascent into the heavens in a vehicle borne by eagles, which is a feature of the Romance. (It was also a popular motif on misericords, pavements and roof-bosses in cathedrals throughout Europe.)[12] This work too has its influence on Gower, who uses stories from it in several passages.[13]

In addition to these two full-length narratives of Alexander's life, there were numerous shorter texts referring to particular episodes in his career. Of these the most widespread were accounts of his adventures in India and beyond, which contribute to the non-military aspect of the medieval Alexander, the sage and seeker after wisdom. There include the *Letter to Aristotle*, Palladius' *On the Brahmans of India* and *The Correspondence of Alexander and Dindimus* (known in Latin as the *Collatio Alexandri et Dindimi*). The *Letter to Aristotle* influenced another late Latin text, the *Letter of Pharasmanes to Hadrian*, which in the later of its several recensions is known as *The Wonders of the East*. The other two texts just mentioned belong to a multifarious tradition about Alexander in India, which dates back to the century after his death and is represented by the Berlin papyrus 13044 (100 BC), containing part of a version of his interview with the Brahmans, and the Geneva papyrus 271 (second century AD), which is the basis of the work by Palladius. Both sets of texts became widely known in East and West and influenced chroniclers such as George the Monk (ninth century AD), whose account of Alexander concentrates on the Indian adventures and Alexander's visit to Jerusalem (a feature prominent in most medieval Greek Alexander books). The Indian and wonder tales were likewise assimilated and recombined in the various recensions of the major Latin version of the Alexander Romance current in the Middle Ages, the *Historia de Proeliis*, which exhibits parts of the *Letter of Pharasmanes* and includes the Brahman episode twice: this became the norm for the numerous European vernacular Alexander Romances based on the *Historia de Proeliis*.

The fourth strand of tradition about Alexander consisted of two texts of Arabic origin, *The Sayings of the Philosophers* and *The Secret of Secrets*. The first of these was composed by Hunayn ibn Ishaq (809–73), incorporating an earlier, simpler version preserved in Syriac, which consists of a series of moralising laments uttered by a series of philosophers, as well as his wife, mother and courtiers, over the dead Alexander. The existence of the Syriac text may suggest that the work has Greek origins,[14] since many Greek works were translated into Syriac in late antiquity. Hunayn's version is much expanded from its model, and consists of a collection of wise sayings attributed to many of the philosophers of antiquity, among whom is included Alexander himself. It was translated into Spanish under the title *Los buenos proverbios* before 1400.[15] A second version of this work, several times longer than Hunayn's, was composed by al-Mubashshir[16] around 1053, and was translated into Spanish (the *Bocados de Oro*) in the late thirteenth century. It also entered the twelfth-century *Disciplina Clericalis* and thence the third recension of the *Historia de Proeliis*. From Latin it was translated also into French. In that form it became the source of the first book printed by William Caxton in England, *The Dictes and Sayings of the Philosophers* (1450). But there are also numerous manuscript versions of the work in English, all differing in some degree one from another.[17]

The second Arabic work, the *Secret of Secrets*, a correspondence between Aristotle and Alexander on the art of kingship, was translated from Syriac by a Christian Arab, Yahya ibn Batrik (900–50). A Hebrew translation was made before 1235 by Yehuda al-Harizi, and a Latin translation not earlier than 1200.[18] (A twelfth-century Spanish translation by Gerard of Cremona and Dominic Gonzalvez was made directly from the Arabic.)[19] A Latin version of Yahya's work was already current by 1200 and is the source of several English works in prose and verse, notably John Lydgate's *Secrees of Old Philisoffres* (Lydgate lived from 1370 to 1449).

This brief sketch will indicate the diversity of material the Middle Ages inherited from antiquity about the heroic figure of Alexander. No satisfactory general study has been made of the texts of the fourth group, which would require the skills of an Orientalist in addition to those of the classical and Middle English scholar. But the student of Middle English literature and of medieval culture in general will find that the Greek and Latin works of the third group, collected in this book, are of direct relevance to the understanding of medieval England's use of the classical heritage.

2 ALEXANDER IN INDIA

To set these legends in a historical context we should say a word about the actual events of Alexander's visit to India. The historical sources for the conquest of India in 327–5 BC are Arrian (5–6), Quintus Curtius Rufus (8. 9ff.) and Plutarch's *Life of Alexander* (57–69).[20] The main outlines of events are clear. Alexander's army, having successfully subdued the region of modern Afghanistan, advanced through the Khyber Pass towards the great city of Taxila, one of the major 'university cities' of ancient India, some thirty kilometres northwest of modern Rawalpindi. Alexander was well received by the ruler of Taxila, who hoped for his help against two neighbouring princes, Abisares and Porus. The former submitted but the latter offered resistance. Alexander had been impressed and interested by the civilisation of Taxila and the presence of numerous ascetics living there on the fringes of the city; he sent one of his staff, the Cynic philosopher and historian Onesicritus, to interview these 'philosophers' and find out about their doctrines. One of them, Calanus, attached himself to Alexander's entourage and later distinguished himself, when he fell ill in Persis, by committing suicide on a blazing pyre. But Alexander could not delay in Taxila, and marched on to fight Porus, whom he successfully defeated in a major battle on the River Hydaspes. Alexander's horse Bucephalus was killed in the battle and buried with honours at a new city-foundation which Alexander named

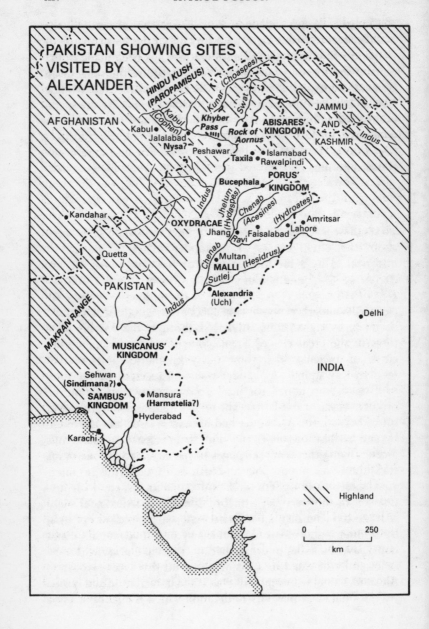

PAKISTAN SHOWING SITES VISITED BY ALEXANDER

Bucephala. Porus, a giant of a man over two metres tall, was captured, offered his loyalty and was confirmed as ruler of the lands beyond the Hydaspes – though now a vassal of Alexander.

Alexander had by now gained information about the lands to the east, in modern India proper, in particular the kingdoms of the Prasii and the Gangaridae based on the Ganges, and conceived ambitions to travel further east and to reach, as he supposed, the Ocean which, according to ancient belief, encircles the world. However, the troops, demoralised by the monsoon rains, mutinied and refused to go further. Alexander conceded defeat and determined instead to follow the Indus to the south and reach the Ocean that way. His course took him through the country of the Oxydracae[21] and thence to the Malli, where Alexander was severely wounded in a foolhardy display of bravery, leaping over the walls of their city into the thick of the fighting. (These two neighbouring peoples seem not to have been very clearly distinguished by the ancient writers, and Arrian adds to the confusion by referring to an attack in the Malli district on a city of the Brahmans (VI. 7), whom he apparently takes to be a people). Further advances brought Alexander to the kingdom of Musicanus and that of Sambus near the Indus delta, at which time he had to cope with revolts in his rear probably fomented by the Brahmans who acted as advisers to the rulers.[22]

Alexander now left India (in modern terms, strictly Pakistan only) behind him and embarked on a dual homeward march to Persis, half the expedition travelling by sea and the rest marching with Alexander through the waterless desert of Gedrosia (Makran).

The historical account of the campaign in India quickly took on a very different form in the legendary compilations about Alexander. The king's frustrated wish to go beyond the Indus into India and towards Ocean became metamorphosed into the story that he actually did penetrate that region. Greek knowledge of India was extremely limited and was based largely on the writings of Ctesias of Cnidus (fifth century BC), who resided at the Persian court and was the author of a book about Persia as well as one about India. Both are unfortunately lost, although there are excerpts and summaries in later writers.[23] What Ctesias said about India is known to us mainly from the summary by Photius the Patriarch of Constantinople (ninth century AD) in his notes of his own reading, plus a few excerpts in Aelian's *Historia Animalium* and one or two other writers. Along with various exotica known also from Herodotus, such as the gold-guarding ants, there is information about the Cynocephali or Dog-headed men, the Pygmies and the Sciapodes (who have just one giant foot, which they use as an umbrella to keep off the sun),[24] and particularly about a great quantity of fabulous beasts (e.g., the manticore) and exotic plants, including the palmyra tree which resembles a giant reed, a river of honey and the trees of the sun and moon which pronounce oracles with a human voice. Much of what Ctesias reported was used by the author of *Alexander's Letter to Aristotle about India*, though he also added a good deal of material of his own.

A second source of information about India was the interview which Onesicritus had conducted with the ascetics of Taxila.[25] It is hard to disentangle from the sources which derive from Onesicritus (which include Plutarch, the Alexander Romance, and the several works on the Brahmans in this volume) exactly how much was in Onesicritus himself and how much was imposed by him on the garbled account he received through the medium of three interpreters; but comparison with what we learn from a later Greek writer on India, Megasthenes, who was the Seleucid ambassador at the court of the Maurya emperor Chandragupta in the second century BC, suggests that Onesicritus did manage to convey some correct information about the ascetics' beliefs and practices.[26] The advice by Calanus (Plutarch, *Life of Alexander*, 65) to hold down the centre of the kingdom, the soundness of which he demonstrates by a practical illustration – treading down an ox-hide, which, as he presses on one side, springs up on the other, and is held flat only when the centre is depressed – intriguingly echoes (with an opposite moral) a story of Chandragupta, who was given advice on how to secure his conquests by an old woman who used the illustration that a chapati is best eaten from the edges inwards rather than from the centre outwards. Perhaps we have here a genuine piece of Indian wisdom preserved in our Greek writers.[27]

The fact that Onesicritus, the Cynic philosopher, had written interestingly about the ascetics of India, with whom the Cynics obviously felt some affinity,[28] prompted the growth of a further literary development of this meeting, in the form of a question-and-answer session between Alexander and the sages. This appears in its earliest form in a papyrus of about 100 BC (Berlin papyrus 13044),[29] and is reused both by the author of the Alexander Romance and by Plutarch.[30] In the Alexander Romance the king appears as a genuine seeker after wisdom and gives the sages presents after they have satisfactorily answered his questions; but in Plutarch the contest is what the folklorists call a Halsrätsel, a riddle on which depends life or death. In the end the sages escape punishment by turning on Alexander a form of the Liar Paradox and thus outwitting him. This part of the encounter did not become established in the later accounts, which concentrate on showing Alexander as learning wisdom from the sages but being unable to make use of it.

In the Hellenistic age the Cynics and the early Stoic philosophers developed a strand of Utopian writing, exemplified by Theopompus' Land of Meropis and, more relevantly for our discussion, the Happy Land of Iambulus located in India and the novel of Euhemerus.[31] These ideal communities represented an antithesis to the busy political life of the Greek city-states, which converged with philosophical controversies about Alexander to produce texts such as the Cynic precursor of Palladius in the Geneva papyrus. Christian reuse of ideas about asceticism informs Palladius' work itself. The contrast of the ways of life of Alexander and the Brahmans is the theme of the Correspondence of Alexander and Dindimus. So in this series of texts we see a steady development from Cynic controversy on Alexander to full-blown Christian apologetic.

Thus the visit of Alexander to India became the occasion for two types of story: an account of the marvels of the East, and a search for the wisdom of the East. Both these aspects were crucial to the development of the character of Alexander in medieval legend, and they were combined with a third which envisaged him seeking to go beyond the limits of the known world to the land of the blessed (or, in Christian terms, paradise). This is the background to the latest of the legends assembled in this book.

Let us look at each of the texts in turn.

3 THE TEXTS

(i) Alexander's Letter to Aristotle about India

There are two Latin texts of the *Letter to Aristotle*. The first belongs to the seventh century at latest; the second is a translation of the first into Italian-Latin dating from the tenth century. (The former has been translated by Lloyd Gunderson; it is the latter which I translate in this book).[32] The Latin is certainly a translation of a lost Greek original which is preserved, in abbreviated form, in several of the recensions of the Greek Alexander Romance attributed to Callisthenes. It appears already in the earliest known version, A, which was compiled not later than 338 AD and maybe several centuries earlier.[33] It is written by Alexander immediately after his conquest of Porus and describes his adventures in India. In the later recensions of the Romance known as epsilon (eighth century) and gamma (ninth century) the adventures it recounts are told in the third person so that they become explicitly a continuation of the story after the conquest of Porus.

As remarked above, much of the material in the letter derives from Ctesias: the giant reeds and the city of reeds;[34] the Dog-heads; the lake of sweet water, which is probably derived from Ctesias' river of honey; the monstrous animals, including the Odontotyrannus, which may be based on Ctesias' giant worms;[35] and the oracular trees of the Sun and Moon.[36] Other elements which specifically relate to Alexander are obviously original to the *Letter*: the city of Porus and Porus' participation in the expedition, and the visit to the Seres or Chinese and the

Valley of Diamonds. Others still derive from common knowledge: elephants and hippopotami, for example. To these the
composer of the *Letter* felt free to add yet more strange
creatures: it would have been dull simply to retail all the same
ones as Ctesias, and once you have started inventing strange
hybrids it is not hard to go on.

The *Letter to Aristotle* was the first Alexander text to be
translated into a medieval language: a translation into Old
English is one of the four texts in the unique codex which
preserves *Beowulf*.[37] The other two texts in this codex are also
concerned with the Far East, the story of St Christopher, and,
more importantly from our point of view, the *Wonders of the
East (De rebus in oriente Mirabilibus)*.[38]

(ii) On the Wonders of the East

This purported to be a letter from Pharasmanes, the King of
Iberia (modern Georgia) to the Emperor Hadrian. There are
several manuscripts with widely varying content; the earliest of
them must have been composed before the year 800. The
manuscript known as D was translated into Old English. This
version is the only one to bring in the character of Alexander in
its discussion of the marvels: allusions to him are absent in the
later versions. The 'letter' draws on earlier Latin lore, notably
the geographer Solinus who in turn assembled most of his
information from the Elder Pliny, as well as from *The Letter of
Alexander to Aristotle*, the *Etymologies* of Isidore and Augus-
tine's *City of God*. It gives brief details of the various strange
beasts and races of men such as the Pygmies, the Sciapodes, the
Dog-heads and others, from which it can be seen that all its
information goes back ultimately to Ctesias. The *Letter of
Pharasmanes*, because of its similarities to the *Letter to Aristotle*,
was pressed into service in the composition of the medieval
Latin versions of the Alexander Romances, first appearing in the
Historia de Proeliis (the first interpolated recension being eleventh century). There were also several French translations of the
letter of Pharasmanes. These in due course contributed, via

Vincent of Beauvais' *Speculum Historiale*, to the account of the marvels of the East in the Book of Sir John Mandeville (1356–7).[39] The influence of these accounts of the Far East can also be seen in pictorial form in several medieval world maps, most notably the Mappa Mundi of Hereford Cathedral.[40]

(iii) The Chronicle of George the Monk

The ninth-century Byzantine chronicler George the Monk, also known as George Hamartolus or George 'the Sinner', included a brief account of the reign of Alexander in his chronicle from earliest times to 842 AD (completed 866–7). It is notable that nearly half of it is devoted to the visit to India, while most of the rest concentrates on Alexander's supposed visit to Jerusalem, in which George draws on the Greek-Jewish historian Josephus and other Jewish sources.

(iv) Palladius, 'On the Life of the Brahmans'

Alexander's encounter with the naked philosophers of Taxila was a feature of all the historical accounts as well as of the Alexander Romance. In the Romance they are referred to not only as 'naked philosophers' but as 'the Brahmans or Oxydor-kai' (i.e., Oxydracae). In fact they may not have been Brahmans at all but some other kind of ascetic, or perhaps Jains (the possibility has even been raised that they might have been Buddhists, but this is unlikely).[41] Whoever they were (and it is my belief that the information about them in the Romance preserves a kernel of historical truth about their beliefs and practices), they quickly became one of the standard features of any description of the East. When Philostratus[42] has his hero, Apollonius of Tyana, visit India, he declares that the Brahmans or Oxydracae whom Alexander met are not the true sages, for these live between the Hyphasis and the Ganges, in a country which Alexander never assailed. This passage shows two things: first, that Philostratus in the third century AD was already acquainted with the legend in the form it takes in the Alexander Romance; and secondly, that the *real* Brahmans had now been relocated to somewhere near the Ganges (which is where Palladius puts them). The terms Brahman and naked philosopher became interchangeable in later antiquity.

The *Life of the Brahmans* is attributed to Palladius,[43] the fifth-century bishop of Helenopolis, and the attribution may very well be correct. In its present form it is certainly a Christian protreptic designed to recommend the monastic life. Palladius states that the second part of his work is an opusculum of Arrian, the historian of Alexander and author of the *Indica*. Now it is a fact that Arrian does once promise a detailed account of the Brahmans but never gives it: could this be his work? If so, it seems inconsistent with his historical principles, which are in general averse to rhetorical elaboration of this kind, and further doubts are raised by the fact that the description of the life of the Brahmans is clearly based on a work partially preserved on a papyrus of the mid-second century AD, in which it appears as one of a collection of Cynic *diatribes*,[44] a form with some similarities to the Christian sermon. It is plain that much of the material in the papyrus is of purely Cynic origin, and as such could have been composed at any time from the second century BC to the second century AD. Arrian, as a pupil of the Stoic philosopher Epictetus, may have shared the Stoics' interest in the Cynic concern with 'the natural life'; but Stoicism is a positive philosophy with more in common with Christianity, in comparison with which the negative attitude of rejection of society by the Cynics can seem superficial or impractical. This Cynic material has been reworked to give it a Christian colour, and in addition there are several references to the games of Rome and the practice of exposing Christians to the wild beasts. An interesting feature is the discourse on vegetarianism. The relevant portion of the papyrus is missing, but the size of the missing part suggests that the treatment of vegetarianism was much briefer in the Cynic text. This passage seems to be an expansion of the material in line with what Christian thinkers believed to have been the practice of the Brahmans (whom they regarded as the ancestors of the sect of Encratites – the self-restrainers).[45]

Palladius' work is preserved in two Greek recensions, of

which I have translated the less elaborate (the *Versio Ornatior* and not the *Versio Ornatior et Elaboratior*).[46] In addition, there are three Latin translations of the work, one of which is falsely attributed to St Ambrose.[47] Palladius' work seems also to have been an influence on the author of the Christian work known as the *Life of Zosimus* and also as the *History of the Rechabites*,[48] which combines details of the Brahmans' way of life with Jewish legends about the land of 'the Blessed' or the sons of Yonadab. The development goes further in the location of the Brahmans on an island (like Paradise) by John of Salisbury, and hence Vincent of Beauvais and Sir John Mandeville.[49]

(v) The Correspondence of Alexander and Dindimus

It is to be assumed that there was a Greek original of this text, which tackles a different aspect of the same theme,[50] Alexander's encounter with the Brahmans, and expands the debate between the two characters on the active and contemplative lives – a kind of early *Allegro* and *Penseroso*. It is not possible to date the Latin text very precisely,[51] though it was referred to in the eighth century by Alcuin, who sent a copy to Charlemagne.[52] This likewise became important in medieval English literature: there is an alliterative verse translation from Gloucestershire of about 1340,[53] known as 'Alexander B', and the section on the Greek gods and their vices is adapted by John Gower.[54] It remained popular for centuries thereafter: there is a chapbook version of 1683.[55]

(vi) Alexander the Great's Journey to Paradise

This is the latest text in the collection, and cannot be dated precisely except to say that it is earlier than 1175, when it was interpolated in the Alexander poem of Pfaffe Lamprecht, also known as the Strassburg Alexander.[56] However, the story it tells is much older. The meeting of Alexander with the old man and the parable of the eye is already in the Babylonian Talmud,[57] and was therefore current before 500 AD. From the Talmud it found its way into the Hebrew versions of the Alexander

Romance,[58] but the course by which it reached Latin cannot be traced (perhaps a Jewish author writing in Latin). The Latin text was the source of a French poem appended to *La Prise de Defur*,[59] one of the thirteenth-century branches of the extremely complicated French *Roman d'Alexandre* tradition. The story of the magic stone also had later reverberations as it contributed to the idea of the Grail, the search for which is the subject of *Parzival* by Wolfram von Eschenbach, who certainly knew this text.[60] The familiarity of the story of Alexander in Paradise to medieval English writers was demonstrated by Mary Lascelles,[61] though it is often barely alluded to. A key text in its transmission was Ranulph Higden's *Polychronicon*, and from him derives Gilbert Hay's story of Alexander's visit to Paradise, a feature which he alone adds to the *Historia de Proeliis* substrate on which he builds.[62]

This completes our survey of the tradition of these five texts and their influence on English literature. In conclusion, it may be worth mentioning the English versions of the Alexander Romance which were familiar alongside these texts and which included the Indian adventures as part of their comprehensive narrative. These include *Kyng Alisaundre* (early fourteenth century),[63] the Alliterative *Romance of Alexander* (mid-fourteenth century),[64] the Thornton Prose Alexander[65] and the *Wars of Alexander*[66] (both fifteenth century), and two Scots versions, the *Buik of Alexander*, probably by John Barbour (1428),[67] and Gilbert Hay's *Buik of Alexander* (1460).[68] The former is essentially a version in Scots of the French *Fuerre de Gadres*; the latter derives from the second interpolated recension of the *Historia de Proeliis*; it is briefer than 'Barbour's' work, which was unknown to Hay.

The following table summarises the chronology of the Alexander texts discussed.

100 BC	Berlin papyrus 13044
1ST C. AD	Geneva papyrus
pre-338	[Greek Letter to Aristotle]
	Julius Valerius

4 ANCIENT CONTROVERSIES ON ALEXANDER

These texts all belong to the continuing history of reactions to, and debates about, the achievement of Alexander and his personality, and can only be understood as growing out of the controversies generated by philosophers and rhetoricians about his career from his own time onwards. What Alexander had accomplished was something far beyond what any Greek had ever conceived of before – not only the conquest of the ancient enemy, the Persian Empire, but the creation of a world empire under Greek-Macedonian rule. From the first, the sheer magnitude of his deeds had stimulated thinkers of all kinds to new efforts to find a place for him in their world views. Where could achievements of this kind be fitted into the traditional moral categories of Greek thought, with their emphasis on the divine punishment of excessive ambition, hostility to 'tyrannical' behaviour and approval of the man who is content with little?

The problem of Alexander found early expression in philosophical and historical writing because Alexander took with him to the East a staff of scholars to record what they saw, and he certainly did correspond with Aristotle, who made use of some of Alexander's ethnographic findings in his own philosophical and scientific studies. The historians approached the subject of his expedition from a variety of perspectives:[69] Ptolemy, the general and the future king of Egypt, wrote a relatively sober and factual account, while Cleitarchus emphasised the wonders and the exotica of the East and Callisthenes was responsible for a semi-hagiographical account in which Alexander could do no wrong – except that his history remained incomplete due to his murder by Alexander when he refused to adopt the oriental custom of prostration before the king. Particularly interesting from our point of view is the contribution of Onesicritus, the devotee of Cynic philosophy who was detailed by Alexander to interview the Brahmans of Taxila, presumably because of his interest in philosophical talk and thought. Onesicritus, as one of Alexander's staff, was the author of a generally favourable, though not always reliable, account of Alexander's adventures. It has often been suspected that in his account of the Brahmans he has to some extent adapted the Indians' ideas, as they were conveyed to him through a series of interpreters, to the dominant opinions of the Cynics, with their rejection of the common opinions of men, of the state and of such fundamental things as clothing, in the interests of a life 'according to nature'. The difference is that the Cynic sought such a life as a way of freeing himself from anxiety, whereas the Brahmans pursued their ascetic mode of life as a way of escaping the world altogether and coming closer to the divine.[70]

In the Romance and other stories about Alexander in India, the interview by Onesicritus was transformed into a direct meeting by Alexander with the Brahmans. No doubt Alexander did meet some of them – not least Calanus, the sage who accompanied him to Persia and there committed suicide by fire – but what they said to each other is not recorded. The early accounts of Alexander's meeting with the Brahmans[71] represent him in a very different light from that which Onesicritus casts on him: here he is a tyrant and his interview has a threatening tone. He tests the philosophers with a series of riddles, and a warning that whoever answers worst will be put to death; the tables are, however, turned on him by the wise men, who defeat the logic of his threats by a form of the Liar Paradox. This story, which is first found in the Berlin papyrus 13044 (cf. pp. 76–7), is taken up by Plutarch as part of his biography, which aims to display the complexity of the great man's character. It is commonly thought that this interview originated as an essay in Cynic philosophy, inspired by the historical meeting but not directly based on it: both the form of the interview – sage encounters tyrant – and the content – paradoxical argument – suit the known approaches of the Cynics and their close colleagues the Megarians.[72] The latter had a special interest in puzzles and paradoxes, which appealed also to the Cynics because of their capacity to annoy people.

A similar Cynic background is present in the famous story of Alexander's encounter with Diogenes at Corinth. Diogenes was the effective founder of the Cynic school and was famed throughout antiquity for his rejection of convention, evinced in his choosing to live in a barrel and in his practice of defecation and masturbation in public (like a dog, hence the name 'cynic'). The story goes that Alexander met Diogenes and was so impressed by his wisdom that he offered him a gift; and Diogenes simply asked Alexander 'Please stand out of my sunshine.'[73] The philosopher content with the bare minimum of natural pleasure is contrasted with the world conqueror for whom no acquisition was sufficient.

Many of the scattered anecdotes from antiquity which show Alexander in a bad light can be traced back to a Cynic milieu or to their Stoic successors. Stoic philosophy was in many respects a development of the moral teaching of Cynicism, with the anti-social elements removed and indeed an insistence that the wise man is not only a king in his own right but also a citizen of a world community.[74] Cicero took from Carneades (a Stoic philosopher) the anecdote of Alexander's encounter with a pirate, in which the pirate remarked that he could see little difference in the moral quality of their respective careers.[75] Another Stoic, Panaetius, compared him unfavourably with his father Philip as a bad ruler.[76] Vanity, arrogance and luxury were leitmotifs of this particular philosophical approach, as well as the view of Alexander as a murderous tyrant – an insane king, in the phrase of the poet Lucan, who filled the world with slaughter and was at last brought down by Fate the Avenger.[77] The horrified emphasis on slaughter was shared also by Lucan's uncle the philosopher Seneca,[78] and it is certainly relevant that both Lucan and Seneca were forced to take their own lives by another tyrannical ruler, the Emperor Nero, who resented their philosophic opposition.

Seneca, however, went beyond mere condemnation to a more complex philosophical position on Alexander's career. In one passage he writes:

> There are some men who, withdrawn beyond the reach of every lust, are scarcely touched at all by any human desires; upon whom Fortune herself has nothing that she can bestow. In benefits I must of necessity be outdone by Socrates, of necessity by Diogenes, who marched naked through the midst of the treasures of the Macedonians, treading under foot the wealth of kings. O! in very truth, how rightly did he seem then, both to himself and to all others who had not been rendered blind to the perception of truth, to tower above the man beneath whose feet lay the whole world! Far more powerful, far richer was he than Alexander, who then was master of the whole world; for what Diogenes refused to receive was even more than Alexander was able to give.[79]

There are several parallels between Diogenes and Dindimus in the Alexander legends. In a fictitious letter of Diogenes[80] the philosopher, on hearing that Alexander wishes to see him, insists that Alexander come to him, not vice versa; just so does Dindimus/Dandamis await the attendance of the king in the Brahman texts. Also interesting is the regular implication of the Diogenes story that Alexander *admired* the philosopher;[81] just so, in the Alexander Romance, Alexander is impressed by Dandamis and gives him gifts, a motif taken up in the Geneva papyrus and its direct descendant, Palladius' *Life of the Brahmans*.

The passage of Seneca just quoted introduces two more of the dominant motifs of ancient thinking about Alexander: his insatiable desire and his fortune. His insatiability, what the historian Arrian termed his *pothos*, 'longing', became a standard element of the characterisation of Alexander, so much so that it was regularly used as a school exercise for training in rhetoric. The *Suasoriae* (Exercises in Persuasion) of the Elder Seneca contain one exercise (1.1) devoted to the theme, 'Alexander debates whether to sail the Ocean'. The elements of the debate are the greatness of the ambition, as commensurate with Alexander's achievements so far, versus the idea that Alexander should be content with what he has already done. In the commentary the rhetorician Cestius is quoted for the view that the topic should be differently treated according to the audience involved, a free people or a king, and among kings according to the ability of the ruler to bear hard truths; in Alexander's case the advice should be well tempered with flattery.

A similar debate is *Suasoriae* 4, 'Alexander the Great, warned of danger by an augur, deliberates whether to enter Babylon'. Here Alexander's debate with himself concludes: 'Shall there be one place in the whole world that has not seen you victorious? Is Babylon closed for the man to whom the Ocean stood open?' Understood is the historical conclusion, in which Alexander did indeed enter Babylon, only to meet his death there – probably from illness, though the Romance attributed it to poison.

Such exercises found their way even into the historians, such as Arrian, who also allows Alexander a debate on whether to sail on to the Ocean beyond the borders of the world. They represented very clearly the image of the overweening conqueror, who in the Romance has repeatedly to be warned by talking birds and other creatures to turn back from travelling beyond the world and from seeking to know the hour of his death. That story too was taken up by the Elder Seneca (*Controversiae* 7.7.19), who refers to the voice heard by Alexander when he debated whether to cross the Ocean, which said, 'How much longer, O unconquered one?' Alexander is regularly used as an exemplum of excessive ambition in the philosophical Letters of the Younger Seneca.[82]

The dangers of ambition had been a leitmotif or commonplace of Greek thought since early classical times: both Aeschylus and Pindar repeatedly descant on the danger for successful heroes of reaching out too far: pride always goes before a fall. The theodicy of Aeschylus' *Agamemnon* erects the progression into a quasi-philosophical system: excess and luxury (both included in the one word *koros*) lead to overweening pride (*hybris*) which then attracts the attention of Fate or Doom (*ate*).[83] For a philosophic mind, Alexander's early death neatly exemplified the truth of this progression.

The question that such success naturally raised was, How did it come about in the first place? What was the reason for Alexander's extraordinary good fortune which made him so puffed up? The question could then be redefined, Was Fortune on Alexander's side or not? The earlier panegyrical historians certainly represented Alexander as a conqueror with the gods on his side. This in itself could be used to belittle Alexander, as it was by Livy, who implied that Alexander made his conquests not by his own abilities but by the favour of Fortune; and 'no man was less able to bear good fortune than Alexander' (Livy 9.18.1). For many thinkers he thus became a type of the tyrant, puffed up by his own good fortune and losing all self-control.[84] Those who admired Alexander had to deal with this objection and attribute his success to his own virtues rather than simply to Fortune. That is the context for the complex discussion in Plutarch's two essays on the subject, *On the Fortune or the Virtue of Alexander*. The arguments are various: Alexander in fact had a great deal of bad fortune too, so surely Fortune was against him much of the time (342C), and his achievements were made in spite of Fortune (328, 341); Fortune gave him his throne, but it is what he did with his position that determines our moral judgement of him (329D); by his virtue he deserved his fortune (340A). His rash behaviour at the Malli town is presented as a contest of Fortune and Virtue (344E).

Integral to Plutarch's discussion is Alexander's own philosophical position. The king is represented as an admirer of Diogenes (331F: 'If I were not Alexander, I should like to be Diogenes'), and even as asking his forgiveness for his mission to conquer the world – just as he almost apologises to Damdamis in the Alexander Romance for his career of conquest, which is forced on him by the necessity of his own nature. The antithesis Plutarch is exploring in this essay is that of the tyrant and the philosopher-king. For the Stoic the true philosopher was in fact a king because he possessed all that he could require, and in Plutarch's view Alexander had been instrumental in creating a world-state of the kind envisaged by the early Stoic thinker Zeno (329AB).

The rehabilitation of Alexander as a king who represented philosophic values became of particular importance in the reign of the Emperor Trajan. The first Roman emperor, Augustus, had drawn some links between his military achievements and those of Alexander, but, as after Augustus the idea of further extending the Roman Empire had been abandoned, Alexander became a largely irrelevant model. Trajan, however, saw himself as (and indeed was) a great military hero, with successful though short-lived conquests of Dacia beyond the Danube and Meso-potamia beyond the Euphrates. It is no accident that the most favourable historical account of Alexander was composed in the reign of Trajan by Arrian, who had held high military office in that emperor's service. Arrian had been a pupil of the Stoic philosopher Epictetus, and showed a particular interest in Alexander's adventures in India and his meeting with the Brahmans, composing a work devoted exclusively to India (the *Indica*) and promising also a monograph on the Brahmans (which does not survive, unless Palladius' monograph, as it states but as seems unlikely, incorporates this work).[85]

Arrian drew on the prevailing Stoic-Cynic tradition in his presentation of the Brahman episode, which is told not in the course of the narrative but in the context of an analysis of Alexander's character, where it is placed in immediate colloca-tion with the Diogenes anecdote. But there is no hint in Arrian of all the regular Cynic objections to Alexander's rule and character, and Arrian is explicit in his admiration of the conqueror for the magnitude of his achievement. Truly the way in which one praised the character of Alexander needed to be modified according to one's presumed audience – in this case, the ambitious conqueror Trajan.

The Trajanic context is even more obvious in the speeches devoted by a contemporary writer, Dio of Prusa (known as Dio Chrysostom, the Golden-Mouthed), to Alexander and his meet-ing with Diogenes. Fortune has deprived us of the eight books of Dio's work *On the Virtues of Alexander*, but two of the

Discourses on Kingship are devoted to Alexander. Oration 4 is a treatment of the interview with Diogenes which presents Alexander as a lover of glory (4) but yet an admirer of the philosopher (7). Alexander is presented as regretting the fate that compels him to arms (9), and only smiles at Diogenes' insults (19–20). Most of the rest of the discourse is devoted to Alexander's inquiry of Diogenes on how to be a good king, and Diogenes' advice:[86] the true king is by definition a good man, and that means achieving self-knowledge, avoiding wealth, pleasure and ambition, and not allowing oneself to be conquered by women (Alexander's sexual continence was a common theme, based on his chivalrous treatment of the women of Darius' family). Dio's Oration 2 develops the idea of Alexander as a philosophic king in the course of a discussion between himself and his father Philip about the value of Homer, his character Achilles as a moral model and the characteristics of the humane king (77). Alexander is represented as having learnt the lessons of kingship from Aristotle (79 – a motif which points the way forward to the extensive development in late antiquity and the Arabic and medieval traditions of Aristotle's advice to Alexander on kingship). Like Plutarch, Dio insists (Oration 64) that Fortune did as much to bring Alexander down as she did to raise him.

An emperor's admiration can do wonders for a man's reputation, and, two centuries after Trajan, Julian (who also died in battle against Persia at the age of 33) liked to see himself not only as a philosopher but as a second Alexander. Julian was a strong admirer of the Cynic philosophy, though not of its more unwashed adherents, who reminded him too much of his *bêtes noires*, the Christian monks. For him, Alexander was a great military hero (II.203) ensnared by Fortune (II.211); and in his curious carnivalesque comedy *The Caesars*, Julian represents Alexander in debate with Roman conquerors such as Caesar and Trajan. Here, while not perfect, his anger and cruelty are tempered by remorse (352B), though his indulgence in pleasure is unfavourably compared with Trajan's austerity. Alexander chooses Heracles as his patron god (335D), as indeed in life he had aimed to follow in the drunken muscle-man's footsteps.

Julian's strange, and perhaps muddled and immature, views of Alexander bring to a close the chapter of responses to his achievement in antiquity. The Cynic view is again to the fore in his thinking, as it will be also in the later independent developments of the Alexander legend in Palladius, the *Correspondence of Alexander and Dindimus*, and so on. But Cynic opposition to Alexander has received an infusion of admiration for the conqueror as one who served the cause of philosophy and just rule as well as arousing the philosophers' ire. Alexander has been constituted as a worthy participant in the debates over the good life; and that is how he enters the Middle Ages, his cruelty and self-indulgence forgotten even as the Greek moral principles that made those traits problematic have been quenched by the different moral concerns of Christianity.

5 THE CHRISTIANISATION OF ALEXANDER

Just what made these texts so popular in the Middle Ages? Or, since that is a question of psychology which can hardly be answered at this distance, How did these texts and the ideas they contain mesh with other features of the medieval world-view?

In the first place, the wonder-tales about India represented an expansion of aspects of a set of texts conveying ideas of world geography as it had been handed down from late antiquity to the Middle Ages. The key point in this development was the development of the circular map, known as the T-O map, which probably goes back to a map commissioned by Julius Caesar.[87] More or less complex versions of this map, representing the three continents arranged around Jerusalem as centre point, and the Mediterranean Sea with the Black Sea and the Nile forming the upright and two arms of a T, are found in many medieval manuscripts, notably those of Sallust's *Jugurtha*. Such a world-view is clearly at the basis of the description of world geography in the *Etymologiae* of the seventh-century bishop Isidore of

Seville, which was the standard text of medieval geography as of much else. This description incorporated the peoples of the East, fabulous beasts and races and the location of Paradise, deriving from the geographer Solinus, who in turn drew his material from the encyclopaedist Pliny, who had read Ctesias and all the other sources. The *Letter to Aristotle* and the *Wonders of the East* represented valuable additional texts to supplement the information given by Isidore without coming into conflict with it. A parallel development took place in the Greek East in the codification of geographical knowledge by writers such as Cosmas Indicopleustes;[88] but the Greek versions of the Alexander texts were apparently no longer current, and so Alexander does not feature as an aspect of ancient geography. (He does, however, become quite important in the Islamic tradition.)[89] The intrinsic fascination and curiosity value of the tales ensured their continuing popularity. It was not until the Far East had been completely opened up by Western embassies to the Mongol Khan that medieval men stopped expecting to find dog-headed and headless men, manticores and monstrous ants on the far side of India.[90]

The second group of texts meshed rather with theological and philosophical concerns. The rhetorical tradition which the Middle Ages inherited from antiquity had already enshrined Alexander as an example (mainly a bad one), and because of his significance it became important to insert him in the Judaeo-Christian tradition. In the Greek East, which drew heavily on the Jewish tradition, Alexander quickly became a pious devotee of the Judaeo-Christian God: in K. Mitsakis's neat phrase, he was born an ancient pagan and died a Byzantine Christian.[91] In the West his character remained ambivalent. Crucial here is the convergence of the figures of the Brahmans with Christian monks and the gradual identification of the island of the Brahmans with Paradise. The first development can be seen in the way Palladius adapts his Cynic source, and the second in the way that the *Life of Zosimus* draws on Brahman lore to describe the Land of the Blessed. The *Correspondence of Alexander and Dindimus* represents a more even-handed approach to the contrast of the two ways of life; at some points at least, Alexander seems to advance sound arguments against the tenets of the Brahmans. However, the *Collatio* was still read as a fundamentally Christian text: Peter Abelard noted his admiration for the figure of Dindimus.[92] The power of this text to stir minds is vividly demonstrated by its re-emergence as a chapbook more than two centuries after its original appearance in Middle English.

The growing importance of the idea of the Earthly Paradise in the medieval consciousness (placed there by Isidore and the Mappae Mundi) lent strength to the stories of Alexander's expedition to the East. Gradually the legendary lands beyond India visited by Alexander came to be identified with the Earthly Paradise; the Oracular Trees became part of its vegetation; and in the popular consciousness the two legends became one:

> After this sir Alysaunder all the worlde wanne,
> Bothe the see and the sonde and the sadde erthe,
> The iles of the oryent to Ercules boundes,
> There Ely and Ennoke ever hafe bene sythen,
> And to the come of Antecriste unclosed be thay never.[93]

The moral standing of Alexander remained contentious. Established as in some sense a philosopher-king by Dio of Prusa and other late classical writers, he entered the Arabic tradition (via Syriac writings, many of them now lost) as a wise man, not least because of his genuinely historical connection with Aristotle.[94] These features of Alexander thus returned to the West when Arabic works were translated into Latin or Spanish, and met head-on the views deriving from classical writings which emphasised both Alexander's liberality[95] and his lechery (his liaison with Candace), his anger (the murder of Callisthenes) and his premature death (seen as a divine judgement). Such features were not incompatible with, though they were not emphasised in, the knightly portrayal of Alexander in the full-length romances in English, French and German, as well as other languages. They lent him a solidity and complexity of character comparable with that of other classical heroes, such as the equally ambiguous Achilles.

But it is the parable of the eye that sets the seal on the Christianisation of Alexander. The central meaning of this story is the vanity of human endeavour, the point put to Alexander by Dindimus and the Brahmans but which he is unable to accept from them. In the story of the eye, the Jewish sage who explains the riddle of the stone clearly presents Alexander with a truth that must be acknowledged. After this, Alexander's death comes as neither surprise nor shame: it represents the reconciliation of the hero with the dictates of the Almighty, which the pagan hero could never achieve. Alexander has become Everyman.

RICHARD STONEMAN

NOTES ON THE INTRODUCTION

1 2361–3. On the medieval Alexander in general, see G. Cary, *The Medieval Alexander* (Cambridge: Cambridge University Press, 1956).

2 See, for example, R. L. Stevenson, *Catriona*, Chapter 10.

3 Edward C. Armstrong, *The Medieval French Roman d'Alexandre*, vols 1–6 (Princeton: Princeton University Press, 1937–76).

4 Cary, op. cit.; D. J. A. Ross, *Alexander Historiatus: A Guide to Medieval Illustrated Alexander Literature* (London: Warburg Institute, 1963).

5 Ulrich von Eschenbach's *Alexandreis* is a vivid illustration of the courtly Alexander.

6 See the translation by John Yardley and Waldemar Heckel (Harmondsworth: Penguin, 1984).

7 Walter of Chatillon, *Alexandreis*, in J. P. Migne, *Patrologiae Cursus Completus*, 209 (1855), 459–574; there is an English translation by R. Telfryn Pritchard (Toronto: Pontifical Institute, 1986).

8 J. Gower, *Confessio Amantis*, iii, 1221ff., 2363ff.

9 *The Greek Alexander Romance*, translated by Richard Stoneman (Harmondsworth: Penguin, 1991).

10 R. Telfryn Pritchard, *The History of Alexander's Battles* (Toronto:

Pontifical Institute, 1992); see also R. Stoneman, in Gareth Schmeling (ed.), *The Ancient Novel* (Leiden: Brill, forthcoming).

11 The House of Fame, 860–1.

12 Chiara Frugoni, 'La leggenda di Alessandro', in F. Sisti, *Alessandro Magno* (Florence: Giunti, 1988).

13 Gower, *Confessio Amantis*, vi, 1789–2366 (Nectanebo); v, 1453ff. (Brahmans); v, 1571ff. and 2543ff. (Candace).

14 There is a very similar work by Eutychius. For what follows here, see Sebastian Brock, 'The laments of the philosophers over Alexander in Syriac', *Journal of Semitic Studies*, 15 (1970), 205–18; Cary, op. cit., 151f.

15 H. Knust, *Mittheilungen aus dem Eskurial* (Tübingen, 1879); texts of both works in Spanish.

16 *Mukhtar al-Hakim*: see Bruno Meissner, 'Mubaššir's Ahbar el-Iskender', *Zeitschrift der Deutschen Morgenländischen Gesellschaft* (1895), 583–627.

17 See Curt F. Bühler, *The Dictes and Sayings of the Philosophers* (EETS 211, London, 1941) for details.

18 I. J. Kazis, *The Gests of Alexander of Macedon* (Cambridge, Mass.: Medieval Academy of America, 1962), 37–9.

19 B. Reilly, *The Medieval Spains* (Cambridge: Cambridge University Press, 1993), 127.

20 The best modern account of Alexander's career is A. B. Bosworth, *Conquest and Empire: the Career of Alexander the Great* (Cambridge: Cambridge University Press, 1988).

21 Arr. 6.4; cf. 11.14; Curt. 9.4. 15ff. Quintus Curtius calls them the Sudracae.

22 This seems the most likely explanation of Arrian's references to the Brahmans: see Bosworth, op. cit., 138.

23 Ctesias is no. 688 in F. Jacoby's *Fragmente der griechischen Historiker* (abbreviated hereafter as *FGrH*). There is a modern French translation, *Ctesias: Histoires de l'Orient* by Janick Auberger (Paris: Les Belles Lettres, 1991).

24 Wilhelm Halbfass, *India and Europe* (New York: SUNY, 1988), 11, suggests that these legendary creatures are a product of the Indian imagination. On Dog-heads, see the exhaustive and exciting book by

David Gordon White, *Myths of the Dog-Man* (Chicago: Chicago University Press, 1991).

25 Strabo 15.1. 63–64. See R. Stoneman, 'Naked philosophers', *Journal of Hellenic Studies* (forthcoming, 1995).

26 Megasthenes: *FGrH* 715; J. W. McCrindle, *Ancient India as described by Megasthenes and Arrian* (Calcutta, Bombay and London, 1877); A. Zambrini, 'Gli Indika di Megastene', *Annali della Scuola Normale di Pisa*, 3, 12 (1982), 71–149; 15(1985), 781–853.

27 R. K. Mookerji, *Chandragupta Maurya and his Times* (4th edn, 1966; repr. Delhi, 1988), 33.

28 Doyne Dawson, *Cities of the Gods* (Oxford: Oxford University Press, 1992); R. Stoneman, 'Who are the Brahmans?' *Classical Quarterly* (forthcoming, 1994).

29 See Appendix 1.

30 See also Boissonade, *Anecdota Graeca*, I, 145ff.; my translation of the Alexander Romance, 131–3.

31 Theopompus: *FGrH* 115. Iambulus: Diod. Sic. II. 57ff. Euhemerus: ibid. V.41–46.

32 Lloyd Gunderson, *Alexander's Letter to Aristotle about India* (Meisenheim am Glan: Anton Hain, 1980).

33 See the Introduction to my translation; note 9.

34 Plin. NH 16.55. 162, deriving from Megasthenes; Klaus Karttunen, *India in Early Greek Literature* (Helsinki: Finnish Oriental Society, 1989), 188–9.

35 Karttunen, op. cit., 190.

36 Ctes. F45. 17, with Karttunen, 220; Gunderson, 111–13.

37 Stanley Rypins, *Three Old English Prose Texts* (EETS, 161, 1924).

38 M. R. James, *Marvels of the East* (Oxford: Oxford University Press, 1929); Rypins, op. cit.; Claude Lecouteux, *De Rebus in Oriente Mirabilibus (Lettre de Farasmanes)* (Meisenheim am Glan: Anton Hain, 1979); there is a translation of the Old English text in Michael Swanton, *Anglo-Saxon Prose* (London: Everyman, 1993), 227–33. See J. Friedman, *The Monstrous Races in Medieval Art and Thought* (Cambridge, Mass.: Harvard University Press, 1981).

39 *Mandeville's Travels*, ed. M. C. Seymour (Oxford: Oxford University Press, 1968).

40 T. P. Wiseman, 'Julius Caesar and the *Mappa Mundi*', in *Talking to Virgil* (Exeter: Exeter University Press, 1992), 22–42; R. Stoneman, 'Romantic ethnography', *Ancient World* (1993); P. D. A. Harvey, *Medieval Maps* (London: British Library, 1993).

41 Friedman, op. cit., thinks they are Parsees; why? See R. Stoneman, 'Naked philosophers', JHS (forthcoming, 1995).

42 Philostratus, *Life of Apollonius of Tyana*, 2.33.

43 Edited by J. D. M. Derrett, 'Palladius de Vita Bragmanorum Narratio', *Classica et medievalia*, 21 (1960), 64–135; and by W. Berghoff, *Palladius: de gentibus Indiae et Bragmanibus* (Meisenheim am Glan: Anton Hain, 1987). See Beverly Berg, 'Dandamis: an early Christian portrait of Indian asceticism', *Classica et medievalia*, 31 (1970), 269–305; R. Stoneman, 'Who are the Brahmans?', *Classical Quarterly* (forthcoming, 1994). The text is earlier than 600 because it is referred to by Isidore, *Etym* 13.2 1.8: see F. Pfister, 'Das Nachleben der Überlieferung von Alexander und den Brahmanen', *Hermes*, 76 (1941), 143–69, repr. in *Kleine Schriften zum Alexanderroman* (Meisenheim am Glan: Anton Hain, 1975), 53–79; the reference is to p. 62 of the latter printing.

44 Victor Martin, 'Un recueil de diatribes cyniques: Pap. Genev. inv. 271', *Museum Helveticum*, 16 (1959), 77–115, with P. Photiades, 'Les diatribes cyniques de papyrus de Genève 271, leurs traductions et élaborations successives', ibid., 116–39.

45 Hippolytus, *Refutatio omnium heresiarum*, 8.7.

46 The terms are Derrett's.

47 A. Wilmart, 'Les textes latines de la lettre de Palladius sur les moeurs des Brahmanes', *Revue Benedictine*, 45 (1933), 29–42, identifies three versions: B, the *Commonitorium*, found in the Bamberg MS; this is an abridgement of V, the Vatican MS; the third is S, the text attributed to Ambrose, an arbitrary recension, probably composed by a humanist. The character Ambrose replaces the narrator, and Moses replaces the Theban scholar.

48 Zosimus, Ante Nicene Fathers 8, 219–24; J. H. Charlesworth (ed.), *The Old Testament Pseudepigrapha* (London: Darton, Longman & Todd, 1983), 2, 443ff.; Chris Knights, 'The "Narrative of Zosimus" or "The History of the Rechabites"?', *Journal of Jewish Studies* (forthcoming).

49 Pfister, op. cit., 73–4.

50 Pfister, op. cit. For a survey of the MSS, see Cary, op. cit., 13f.

51 Found in the tenth-century Bamberg MS, which also includes the *Commonitorium* and second *Latin Letter to Aristotle*.

52 Cary, op. cit., 14, who dates the first version to the fourth century.

53 MS CCC (Cambridge) no. 219, ed. Bisse; ed. W. W. Skeat, EETS extra series 31 (1878). It is usually known as Alexander B: see Appendix 2 for an extract. W. R. J. Barron, *English Medieval Romance* (London: Longman, 1987), 124.

54 *Confessio Amantis*, v. sect. 2. See Appendix 2.

55 *The Upright Lives of the Heathens briefly noted* . . ., published by Andrew Soule (1683); see Appendix 2.

56 Cary, op. cit., 19.

57 Talmud, Tamid 32b.

58 I. J. Kazis, op. cit.

59 Ed. A. Hilka in L. P. G. Peckham and M. S. La Du, *La Prise de Defur* (Princeton: Princeton University Press, 1935).

60 Henry Kratz, *Wolfram von Eschenbach's 'Parzival'* (Berne, 1973), excursus EE 'lapsit exillis', 590–3.

61 Mary Lascelles, 'Alexander and the Earthly Paradise in medieval English writings', *Medium Aevum*, 5 (1936), 31–47, 79–104, 173–88. See also Arturo Graf, 'La leggenda del paradiso terrestre', in *Miti, Leggende e Superstizioni del Medio Evo* (Milan: Mondadori, 1984), 134–8.

62 Gilbert Hay, *Buik of Alexander*, 16182–16315. See Appendix 2.

63 *Kyng Alisaundre*, ed. G. V. Smithers, I and II (EETS 227, 1952 and 237, 1957).

64 The Alliterative *Romance of Alexander*, ed. J. Stevenson (London, 1849).

65 *The Prose Life of Alexander from the Thornton MS*, ed. J. S. Westlake (EETS 143, 1931).

66 *The Wars of Alexander*, ed. H. N. Duggan and T. Turville-Petre (EETS SS 10, 1989).

67 [John Barbour] *Buik of Alexander*, ed. R. L. G. Ritchie (Aberdeen: Scottish Text Society, 4 vols, 1921–9).

68 Gilbert Hay, *The Buik of King Alexander ye Conqueror*, ed. John

Cartwright, vols 'ii' and 'iii' (Aberdeen: Scottish Text Society, 4th ser., 16 and 18, 1986–90).

69 L. Pearson, *The Lost Histories of Alexander the Great* (Chicago: Scholars Press, 1983); W. Hoffmann, *Das literarische Porträt Alexanders des Grossen* (Leipzig, 1907).

70 On this, see R. Stoneman, 'Naked philosophers', *Journal of Hellenic Studies* (forthcoming, 1995); 'Who are the Brahmans?', *Classical Quarterly* (forthcoming, 1994).

71 Berlin papyrus 13044; see U. Wilcken 'Alexander de Grosse und die indischen Gymnosophisten', *Sitzungsberichte der preussischen Akademie zu Berlin* (phil.-hist. Klasse) (1923), 150–83; Plutarch, *Life of Alexander*; T. S. Brown, *Onesicritus* (Berkeley: University of California Press, 1949), 71.

72 Stoneman, *Journal of Hellenic Studies* (forthcoming, 1995).

73 Arr. *Anab* 7.2; Diog. *Ep* 33.

74 Doyne Dawson, *Cities of the Gods* (Oxford, 1992).

75 Cic. *Rep* 3.14.24; taken up by Jewish writers: see J. ben Gorion, *Der Born Judas* (Leipzig; Insel, n.d.), 183.

76 Cic. *de officiis* 1.90 and 2.53.

77 *Phars* 10.20–46.

78 Sen. *Ep* 94.62.

79 Sen. *de ben* 5.4.

80 Diog. *Ep* 23; cf. Julian 212c.

81 Julian 212c; Dio Chr. Plut 33F.

82 Seneca *Ep* 53.10, 59.12, 83.19.

83 Aesch. *Ag* 380 ff. Julian 199A applies the principle to Alexander.

84 For Timaeus' view of Alexander, see Hoffmann, op. cit., chapter 2; Menander fr. 924.

85 See above, p. xxi.

86 Cf. also Diog. *Ep* 40 on how to rule: self-knowledge and the keeping of good company.

87 T. P. Wiseman, op. cit.; Stoneman, 'Romantic ethnography', *Ancient World* (1994).

88 *Cosmas Indicopleustes*, ed. E. O. Winstedt (Cambridge: Cambridge

University Press, 1909); trans. J. W. McCrindle, *The Christian Topography of Cosmas, an Egyptian Monk* (Hakluyt Society 98, 1897).

89 On Islamic geography, see in general A. Miquel, *La géographie humaine du monde musulman jusqu'au milieu du 11e siècle*, vols 1–3 (The Hague: Mouton, 1975).

90 J. R. S. Phillips, *The Medieval Expansion of Europe* (Oxford: Oxford University Press, 1988), esp. chapter 7.

91 K. Mitsakis, *Der Byzantinische Alexanderroman nach dem Code Vindob. Theol. Gr. 244* (Munich: Institut für byzantinische und neugriechische Philologie der Universität München, 1967), 18.

92 Cary, op. cit., 93.

93 *Parlement of the Thre Ages*, 332–6. Brilliantly explicated by Mary Lascelles, op. cit.; cf. Arturo Graf, op. cit.

94 Cary, op. cit., 105ff.

95 A Stoic tradition: Cary, op. cit., 85ff.

ABBREVIATIONS

The following are used in the references for this edition.

Aesch: Aeschylus (*Ag*: *Agamemnon*)

AJ: *Antiquitates Judaeorum*

Arr.: Arrian (*Anab*: *Anabasis*)

Cic.: Cicero (*Rep*.: *Republic*)

Ctes.: Ctesias

Curt.: Quintus Curtius

Diog: Diogenes (*Ep*: *Epistles*)

Dio. Chr.: Dio Chrysostom

Diod. Sic.: Diodorus Siculus

EETS: Early English Text Society

FGrH: *Fragmente de griechischen Historiker*

Isid.: Isidore (*Etym*: *Etymologiae*)

JHS: *Journal of Hellenic Studies*

Phars: Lucan, *Pharsalia*

Plin. NH: Pliny, *Natural History*

Plut.: Plutarch

Sen.: Seneca (*Ep*: *Epistles*; *de ben*: *de beneficiis*)

Val. Max.: Valerius Maximus

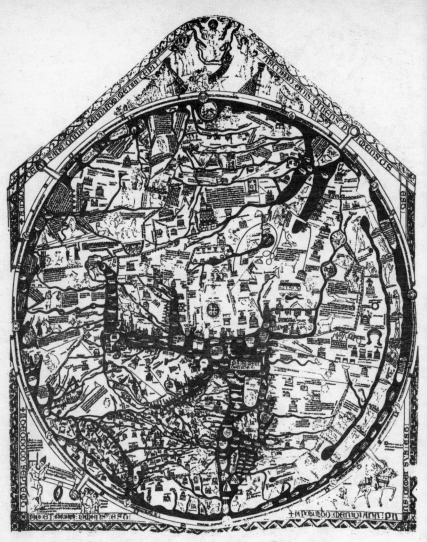

The Hereford Mappa Mundi is the largest and best-preserved
medieval map in the world and was the work of Richard of
Haldingham who became Prebend of Norton near Hereford soon
after 1276. The form of the map is that of the so-called T-O maps, in
which the Mediterranean and Black Sea form a T within the circle of
the whole. Jerusalem is in the centre and the earthly paradise is at the
top. The geography of the regions east of Jerusalem, and the various
peoples shown, are derived from fabulous accounts of the east contained in the Alexander legends and related antique and early
medieval texts.

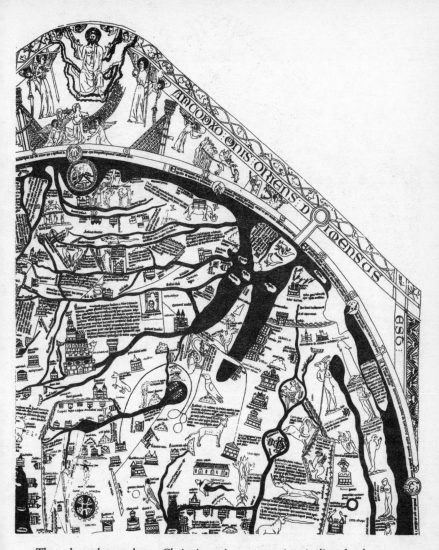

The enlarged area shows Christ in majesty at top (east), directly above the Earthly Paradise (an island in the encircling Ocean). Below the Paradise are the four rivers of Paradise and the tall tower of Babylon. The four rivers run through India, which is bordered on the south-west by the Red Sea (coloured red on the original).

LEGENDS OF
ALEXANDER THE GREAT

I
Alexander's Letter
to Aristotle about India

My dear master,

1 I hold you more dear than any except my mother and my
sisters, I think of you always even when I am in critical situations
in the midst of battle. Since I know that you are interested in
philosophy, I thought I would write to you about the parts of
India, and the kinds of serpents, men and beasts that are to be
found there: whenever a man learns something about a new
subject, it increases his learning and his understanding. Although
your wisdom is already great, and your learning needs no
support from any new knowledge, nevertheless, because of your
love of me I would like to write to you about the things I saw in
India during the arduous and dangerous journey of the Macedonians: I want you to know what I have been doing and I want
there to be nothing that is not known to you. I would not have
believed there could be so many wonders on the earth if I had
not seen them first with my own eyes. Truly marvellous is
mother earth, who brings to birth many things both good and
bad, including plants and animals in so many different forms.
Even if a man could see all those things it would hardly be
possible for him to learn all their names, so many and various
are they.

First I shall tell you about the things I saw, lest it should be
said that all this is a fable and I am a liar. You, who were my
teacher, know what I am like and how I have always kept to the
limits of propriety and have always described things in less
extravagant terms than the reality. Now, I hope, you will
understand that I do not relate these things for the sake of my
own glory; I would rather they had been less, because they

would have cost us less labour in discovering those things which we did discover. I must thank the young men of Macedonia and all our army for enduring so many hardships to win me the name of king of kings. I know, dear master, that you rejoice in my glory, and it would be a fault in me if I did not write to you or to my mother Olympias and my sisters concerning everything that is of value in my dominions, since I consider that everything that benefits me is common property with you and them also. In my earlier letters I described to you the settings of the sun and moon and stars, and other celestial bodies, all of which I measured with great care and sent to you; and whenever there was something new to tell I wrote it down on paper, so that, when you read it, you will know what care Alexander could take over such matters.

2 In the month of May, after we had conquered Darius the King of the Persians at the river called Granicus,[1] we subjugated all his realm to ourself, and placed our nobles in the provinces of the East. We enriched ourself with all Darius' wealth, as I described in my earlier letter. I do not wish to repeat myself, and will not go over again what you know already.

In the month of July, we reached the part of India called Fasiace,[2] where we overcame King Porus with great speed, and enriched ourself with his abundant wealth. I think it right, lest it be forgotten, that I should write of the enormous size of his army, which included, besides foot soldiers, 14,800 chariots, all armed with scythes, and 400 elephants which carried towers in which armed men stood ready to fight. We captured the city of Porus and his house[3] in which there were 400 golden columns with golden capitals; the walls of the palace were also covered with gold plates of the thickness of a man's finger: I had cuts made in these plates in several places. There was also a golden vine, with golden leaves, hanging between the columns: its branches were of crystal, studded with rubies and emeralds. In fact all the rooms were decorated with the jewels known as pearls, as well as drop pearls and carbuncles. The throne room was of ivory, and it had false beams of the wood known as ebony, a dark wood found in India and Ethiopia; while the other chambers were of cypress wood. Outside the palace there were statues of gold, and golden plane trees, and in their branches were many kinds of birds of various colours, with golden beaks and claws, and small and large pearls in their ears. We also found many vessels of gems and crystal there, but not much silver.

3 After I had got possession of all this, I wanted to see the interior of India, so I marched with my army to the Caspian Gates.[4] There I was impressed by some land which seemed good, while other areas appeared most disagreeable. In the same regions there were serpents and wild beasts, which lived in the valleys and plains, in the woods and the mountains. The people of that land told us that we should be much troubled by beasts and serpents.

Still, I wanted to pursue King Porus, who had fled from the battle, before he reached the open spaces of the desert. I took with me 150 guides, who knew the way. It was the month of August, and our way lay through sandy wastes under the burning sun. I promised rewards to those who should lead me safely through the unknown regions of India, if they could bring me safe to Bactria with all my army. In that region there is a people called the Seres, and trees grow there which have leaves like wool, which the local people collect to make clothes for themselves.[5] Even our guides started collecting some of that wool. As far as I could understand it, our guides wanted to conduct us through regions of deadly danger, where there were quantities of serpents and wild beasts and monsters.

When I realised this, I said that it was partly my fault, because I had disregarded the advice of my friends and of the men of the Caspian region, who had told me that this was not the way to a quick victory. I ordered my soldiers to arm themselves fully, for I was afraid that enemies might take us by surprise and take away the wealth of gold and jewels which my soldiers were carrying. They had also become so rich that they could hardly carry their own gold; in addition, they were severely weighed down by their weapons: I had had all of these plated with gold, so that the whole army shone like the stars. The sight of that army was truly amazing, so far did it excel all other peoples both in bravery and in its adornment. I was delighted both at my good fortune and at the sight of my large and noble army.

However, it commonly happens that when a man achieves some success, this is pretty soon followed by adversity; and we now began to suffer from severe thirst. When we could no longer endure the torment, a soldier named Zefirus discovered some water in a hollow rock; he filled his own helmet with it and brought it to me, being more zealous for my life than for his own. Then I called together the whole army and in the sight of them all I poured away the water.[6] I thought that if the army saw me drinking it would only make them feel even more thirsty. I praised the generosity of Zefirus towards me, and gave him a generous gift. What I did with that water encouraged the whole army, and we began to move again.

4 As we continued on our way, I saw not far off a river flowing through the desert, on the banks of which were reeds 60 feet high and thicker than a pine tree; in fact they were used for making beams in the natives' houses.[7] At once I had the army pitch camp, because the men and the animals were suffering so severely from thirst. But when they went to drink at the river, they found the water as bitter as hellebore (or velatrum as it is commonly called);[8] so neither men nor animals could drink it without pain. I was more distressed about the animals than for our own discomfort, since I know that men are more able to endure hardship than animals. I had with me a thousand elephants to carry the gold, and 400 scythed chariots with four horses to each chariot, and in addition 200 ordinary chariots with two horses apiece. We had 2,000 horsemen with us, 250,000 foot soldiers, and almost 2,000 mules to carry the belongings of the army and of the people, as well as 2,000 camels, dromedaries and oxen to carry the food. In addition there was a great quantity of oxen, cows and sheep for consump-

tion. Many of the horses, elephants and mules had golden harness.

The poor cattle could not contain themselves in the face of their thirst; even the soldiers began to lick iron, or to drink oil; others were in such a state that they drank their own urine. For this reason I was extremely distressed, and more concerned about my people than about myself. I ordered all the armed men to follow me, and made it clear that I should punish anyone whom I should find unarmed. Everyone was astonished that it should be necessary to bear arms when they were so thirsty and there was no enemy in sight. But I knew that we had to travel through regions full of beasts and serpents.

5 So we followed the bank of the aforementioned river with the bitter water, and at the eighth hour we came to a castle which stood on an island in that river and was built out of the reeds which I mentioned before. There we saw a few naked Indians who immediately hid themselves when they saw us. I wanted to speak with them and to get them to show me where to find water. But when none of them showed themselves, I gave orders to fire a few arrows into the castle, to frighten them into coming out since they would not do so voluntarily. But they only retreated further in their fear. Then I sent 200 of my Macedonian soldiers into the river, lightly armed.

They had swum about a quarter of the way across when suddenly a new shock assailed us. We saw emerging from the deep a number of hippopotamuses, bigger than elephants. They are called hippopotamuses because they are half men and half horses.[9] We could only watch and wail as they devoured the Macedonians whom we had sent to swim the river. I was angry at the guides who had brought us to such a place, and I ordered a hundred of them to be despatched into the river. Then the hippopotamuses began to swarm like ants and devoured them all. Because we did not want to have a night battle with the hippopotamuses, we departed from the place.

6 When it came to the eleventh hour, we saw in the middle of the river some men in little round boats made of reeds. We

asked them where we might find fresh water. They told us in their language that we should need to find a certain lake of sweet water, to which they undertook to guide us. We marched all night, exhausted by thirst, and suffering under the weight of our weapons. Then another trial was added to our troubles: numbers of lions, bears, leopards and tigers came to meet us, and we spent all night fighting them. We were very tired the next day; it was already the eighth hour when we reached the lake. But when we had drunk of the sweet water, we cheered up: there was enough to drink for all the army and the animals. Then I ordered the men to pitch camp, three miles in length and breadth. We had to cut down much of the forest which surrounded the lake (which was about a mile across). We placed our elephants in the central part of the camp, so that the army could easily defend itself if anything should attack us in the night. The men lit 1,500 fires, since we had plenty of wood from the surrounding forest.

7 At the eleventh hour I had the trumpet sounded, and I ate my meal and ordered all my companions to eat theirs. About 2,000 golden lamps were lit. When the moon began to rise, scorpions suddenly arrived to drink in the lake; then there came huge beasts and serpents, of various colours, some red, some black or white, some gold; the whole earth echoed with their hissing and filled us with considerable fear.

I had shields placed in order before the camp, and we held in our hands long spears, to deal with any serpents that approached us. We killed some of them in the fires: it was a regular battle with those serpents. When the serpents had drunk from the lake, they began to depart, which pleased us greatly. It was already the third hour of the night, and we were hoping that we should now get some sleep, when more serpents arrived. These had crests on their heads and were thicker than columns. They came down from the nearby mountains and likewise made for the water. They moved with their breasts erect and their mouths open, and darted venom from their eyes; their breath too was poisonous. We spent more than an hour of the night fighting with them, and they killed of our party 30 servants and 20 soldiers. I asked the Macedonians not to let their courage fail them in this danger. After the serpents had gone away, there arrived crabs with hard backs like those of crocodiles, and when we threw our spears at them they did not penetrate; still, we killed a good many of them with fire, while others retreated into the lake.

It was now the fifth watch of the night and we wanted to rest; but now white lions arrived, bigger than bulls; they shook their heads and roared loudly, and charged at us; but we met them with the points of our hunting spears and killed them. There was great consternation in the camp at all these alarms. The next creatures to arrive were enormous pigs of various colours;[10] we fought with them too in the same way. Then came bats as big as doves with teeth like those of men; they flew right in our faces and some of the soldiers were wounded.

8 The next arrival was a beast larger than an elephant, with three horns on its forehead. In the Indian language it was called Odontotyrannus or tooth-tyrant.[11] It looked a bit like a horse and its head was black. It was about to drink from the lake, when it suddenly saw our camp and made a charge at us. I positioned some Macedonians to resist it. But it killed 24 of them and trampled another 52; then we managed to kill it. Then there arrived shrews bigger than foxes; any of our animals which they bit died instantly, but for men their bite was harmful but not deadly. As dawn approached, there came birds like vultures but red in colour with black feet and beaks.[12] They did not harm us, but they filled the entire bank of the lake and began to catch fish and eels from the water and eat them. They did not attack us, nor we them. Then I was angry at the guides who had brought us to this dreadful place. I had their legs broken and left them to be eaten alive by the serpents. I also had their hands cut off, so that their punishment was proportionate to their crime.

9 Then I encouraged my soldiers to be brave and not to give up in adversity like women. The trumpet sounded, and we struck

camp, since the barbarians and Indians had gathered together and were planning a new attack on us. My soldiers, however, were in the best of spirits and anticipated the same victory and success as we had achieved previously. We left the dangerous place and marched along a good road, full of gold and other riches; the men of the region received us kindly. We halted for 20 days to allow the army to recuperate; then we marched in another seven days to the place where Porus was encamped with his combined army, ready for battle.

He wanted to know about me and interrogated my soldiers about my whereabouts and what I was doing. Then my soldiers told him, 'We do not know what Alexander is doing'; then they came and told me that Porus had been questioning them. When I heard that, I took off my royal robes and put on a soldier's uniform. I pretended I was going to the castle to fetch wine and meat. When Porus saw me, he had me brought to him and interrogated me about what Alexander was doing and how old he was. I lied to him and said, 'As for his age, I know that he is an old man, and he is probably sitting by the fire, as old men are wont to do.' Then Porus was very pleased at the thought of doing battle with an old man, since he himself was young. He rose up in delight and said, 'Why does he not recognise that he is old? Why does he want to fight with a young man?' I said to him, 'I do not know what is in Alexander's mind; I am just a shepherd belonging to one of the Macedonian soldiers.' Then Porus gave me a letter full of threats to give to King Alexander, and promised me a reward. I promised to carry out his request and said, 'You may be sure that this letter will reach the hands of Alexander.' Immediately I returned to the camp. I laughed a lot both before I had read the letter and afterwards. I am sending you, dear master, a copy of that letter, and also to my mother and sisters, so that you can marvel at the pride and presumption of that barbarian.

10 Then I fought a battle with the Indians and defeated them, as I had hoped. I assumed the throne which Porus had held, and then I returned it to him. When he realised that I was returning

his kingdom to him, he showed me his treasuries, which I had not known about, and I made myself, my companions and the whole army rich from them. Then King Porus became an ally of the Macedonians, to whom he had previously been hostile. He led me to a place where there stood statues of gold which had been erected by Father Liber (Dionysus) and Hercules,[13] who are gods among the pagans. I wanted to know if they were of solid metal, so I had holes drilled in all of them. When I found that they were all solid, I had the holes refilled with gold. When we left that place there was nothing new to see but deserted plains, forests and mountains over against Ocean, where they said that elephants and serpents lived. However, we marched on to the sea, to find out whether we could sail round the earth via Ocean,[14] and since the men of that region said that that was a region of darkness, and that Hercules and Father Liber had not dared to advance so far, I gave orders that we should circumnavigate the leftward part of India. I wanted there to be no place that remained unknown to me, and that Porus should hide none of his kingdom from me.

11 We came to a dried-up marsh which was full of reeds. When we tried to cross it, a new kind of beast came out of it: it had as it were a saw on its back, and resembled a hippopotamus though its chest was like a crocodile's and it had very powerful teeth. It swiftly killed two of our soldiers. We succeeded in transfixing it with our spears, but were only able to kill it with iron hammers.

12 Horrified by this new creature we had seen, we proceeded from there to the most distant forests of India. We pitched camp near a river called Buemar; it occupied an area six miles long and two wide. It was the eleventh hour of the day and we were ready to eat; but suddenly there arrived a shepherd and some wood-carriers to tell us that a herd of elephants was approaching us from the forest. I ordered some of the Thracian horsemen to ride and take some pigs with them to meet the elephants: for I knew that elephants hate the sound of pigs squealing. I sent after them some more horsemen and all the trumpeters; we stationed the rest of the foot soldiers in the camp. Then I set off

with Porus and the rest of the horsemen. We saw a herd of elephants pointing their trunks at us (these are like large teeth in their cheeks)[15]. Their backs were black, white and red. Porus said that we should be able to overcome the elephants if the pigs which the horsemen had brought could be made to keep squealing. This we did, and when the elephants heard the sound of the trumpets and the squealing of the pigs, they ran away. The horsemen then pursued them, hamstrung a good many and killed 980. They took their teeth and horns and brought them back to the camp. Then I ordered a trench and a stockade to be built right around the camp, to prevent the elephants or any other beasts coming in the night and harming us. After that we had a quiet night and slept till daybreak.

13 On the next day we set off for another part of India. As we went along, we came upon broad plains where we saw men and women whose bodies were hairy like those of beasts. [The Indians call them the Fish-eaters.][16] They were naked and had long feet, and they were able to live equally in the rivers or on the ground. When we tried to approach them, they immediately dived into the river.

After that we came to a forest full of Dog-headed men. When they tried to attack us we drove them off with arrows. (They are called Cynocephali because they have the heads of dogs.)[17] We now entered a desert region where the Indians who accompanied us told us that we should find nothing new that was worth seeing.

14 We made now to return to Fasiace, where we had come from. I told the army to extend the camp over 12 miles so that we should be close to water. We had put up all our tents and lit a number of fires when suddenly the wind began to blow from the east, knocking down all the tents, and sending sparks and embers from the fires flying, falling on the animals and burning them, which caused them much distress. I comforted the soldiers by explaining that the storm was not the result of the anger of the gods against us but was a result of the season, which had reached the equinox. We picked up all the materials which the

wind had scattered and found a sheltered valley to re-establish our camp. After everything was organised I ordered the soldiers to eat; the wind had fallen but it was getting very cold. Snow began to fall in huge flakes like lumps of wool. I was afraid that snowdrifts would build up in the camp and ordered the soldiers to tread down the snow. We were greatly aided in this by the quantity of fires we had lit, although some of them were put out by the snow. One thing which helped us was that it soon stopped snowing and came on to rain. At once the sky was covered with dark clouds, and we saw burning clouds like torches descending from the sky, so that the whole plain blazed with their fire. My soldiers were afraid to say to me that this was the result of the anger of the gods because I, a mere mortal, had tried to go where even Hercules and Father Liber had not gone. I ordered the soldiers to use torn clothing to put out the fires that were blazing on the ground. Soon our prayers were answered and the storm abated; we had the camp fires lit again, but thick clouds continued to cover the sky and for three days we saw no sight of the sun for the dense cloud. We buried 500 soldiers who had died in the snow, and moved away from the place.

15 [So we saw the high mountain ranges and the Ocean in Ethiopia.] The next thing we saw was [the Nysaean Mountains and] a cave where Father Liber lay sleeping. We were told that if anyone entered that cave he would die of fever within three days. Some men I sent there were lost and that was how we discovered that this was really the case. I began to beseech the gods to allow me, the king of all the world, to return victorious to Macedonia and my mother Olympias. But I knew that my prayer was in vain. Then I asked the Indians who accompanied me whether there was any particular wonder that we still ought to see. They all insisted that there was nothing else to be seen. So we made our way back to Fasiace.

16 Then two old men came to meet us. We asked them if they knew of any new things which we ought to see. They told us that they knew of something very wonderful which they would

show us, but that the journey would be long – ten days' marching – along a tricky path full of serpents and broken by water. I replied kindly to these old men and asked them what great and noble thing it was that they were promising to show us.

'You will see two trees,' one of the men replied cheerfully, 'that of the Sun and that of the Moon. The tree of the Sun [is male and] speaks the Indian language and the tree of the Moon [is female and] speaks Greek.[18] From them you will be able to learn all the good and evil things that are going to happen to you.'

When I heard about these incredible trees, I at first thought they were joking. I had them beaten up and subjected to indignities, saying to them, 'Has my glory spread from east to west simply for me to be mocked by old men like that?' But the old men insisted on oath that they were not deceiving me and that they could demonstrate the truth of what they said. My friends and companions begged me not to pass up the opportunity of going to see these trees.

I took with me 300 horsemen and sent the rest of the army with a few company commanders and King Porus, and all the goods, to Fasiace. Then we set off with our picked troops, under the guidance of the old men. As they had warned us, the way was tricky and led through hard places, until we finally came to the place where the trees were. We saw many serpents and wild beasts: I do not describe these to you because they had names only in the Indian language.

17 When we drew to the place to which the old men were leading us, we saw women and men dressed in skins. When we asked them who they were, they said they were Indians. When we came to the place where the trees were, we saw a large open space. There were many frankincense and balsam trees there, almost enough to be called a forest: the local people used to eat their fruit. We entered the sacred precinct and saw the high priest, who was over ten feet tall, with black skin, pointed teeth

like a dog's, and pierced ears with jewels suspended from them. He greeted me and asked me why I had come.

'I have come to see the sacred trees of the Sun and Moon', I said.

Then the barbarian replied, 'If you are unpolluted by intercourse with woman or man, you may enter the holy place.'

My 300 companions entered with me. The priest ordered us to take off our rings, clothes and shoes; we obeyed and did as he commanded.

It was the eleventh hour of the day and the priest was waiting for sunset, at which time, he said, the tree of the Sun would make its utterance. Similarly, the tree of the Moon would utter at moonrise. I was sceptical and thought this unlikely to be true.

18 We began to advance through the wood, which was surrounded by high walls. We saw the balsam flowing in abundance from the branches of the trees. My companions and I began to strip pieces of bark from the trees, because their fragrance was so sweet. In the centre of the wood were two trees resembling cypress trees, about a hundred feet tall. I was most impressed by their size and remarked to the priest that they must have needed a lot of rain to grow so tall; but the priest said that it never rained in that place, and furthermore that no beast, bird or reptile ever entered its bounds, because it had been since antiquity consecrated by the Indians to the Sun and Moon. I wanted to make a sacrifice, but the priest would not allow me, saying that it was forbidden in that place either to pour incense or to kill any animal. He instructed me instead to kiss the trees and to ask the Sun and Moon to make prophetic utterances. I asked the priest if the trees would speak to us in Greek or in Indian.

'Both,' he replied; 'but the tree of the Sun will first foretell the future in Indian, while the tree of the Moon will start to speak in Greek and conclude in Indian.'

19 Soon afterwards we saw the rays of the sun gleaming through the branches above us, and the priest said, 'Rise, look at the trees, and ask silently what each of you wants to know;

but pose your question only in your heart, and do not speak out loud.' Then we began to peer about intently in case there might be a jackdaw or a parrot hidden in the branches, as these birds are able to speak, as it were, in a human voice. But we could see no such trickery hidden in the branches of the trees. I began to wonder if I would return in triumph to my country and to my mother Olympias and my dear sisters. Suddenly one of the trees began to speak in the Indian tongue.

'As for the question you have put to me, Alexander, you will be lord of all the world. But you will not return alive to your country, as the fates have decreed otherwise for you.'

As I did not know which of the trees this was, I asked the Indians I had brought with me to interpret its words for me: they told me that it was the tree of the Sun. My friends began to lament at its answer – they were three of my most faithful companions, Perdiccas, Clitus and Philotas – because there was no man I feared, and there was no need for me to fear any man in that place where killing was unlawful.

We moved on and as evening fell we prepared to question the tree of the Moon; but the moon had not yet risen. Presently we entered the same sacred spot, stood beside the tree of the Moon, prayed, and I asked where I was to die. Just as the moon's rays touched the top of the tree, the tree spoke and addressed me in Greek.

'Alexander, you have fulfilled your span of life, and this very year, in the month of May, you will die in Babylon, betrayed by one of whom you least suspect it.'

I began to weep, and so did my friends. But it did not occur to me that any of them would betray me, since they were all prepared to die to save me. We left the place: my heart was very sorrowful and I had no appetite for food. My friends begged me not to be cast down and make myself faint with not eating; so, against my own inclination, I ate a little and positioned myself in the sacred place to await the sunrise.

The next day I got up at first light and roused my companions. The priest was lying down wrapped in skins, and before him was a clay dish of frankincense on an ivory tray, left over from his meal. There was also a knife [of ivory], since [they lack] bronze, iron, lead and silver, but they have plenty of gold. They eat frankincense and balsam and drink the water which flows from the nearby mountain. We woke the priest and entered a third time to question the trees.

'Tell me', I said, 'most holy tree, by whose hand I am to die and what sort of death will come to my mother and my sisters.'

The tree answered in Greek, 'If I tell you who is to kill you, you will kill him in order to change the decree of fate concerning you, and the three Sisters, Clotho, Lachesis and Atropos, will be angry at me for hindering the fulfilment of their decision. You will die in one year and eight months in Babylon, not by the sword as you suppose, but by poison. Your mother will die an ignominious death, and will not be buried, but the birds and beasts will devour her.[19] However, for this short time you will be lord of all the world. Now, do not question us further, but leave this place and return to Porus in Fasiace.'

Then the priest also commanded us to leave, as the trees were being annoyed by our weeping and wailing. So I addressed all my soldiers and announced that we were returning to Porus in Fasiace; but I instructed the soldiers who had been with me to say nothing of the oracles I had received in answer to my questions about my life, but to keep it all secret in their hearts.

20 From there we advanced to the valley of Jordia, where there were serpents which had on their necks stones known as emeralds.[20] These serpents will not allow anyone to approach this valley. They live on asafoetida and white pepper. Every year they fight a battle and many of them are killed. From there we took away only a few emeralds, but quite large ones. Then we went through many terrible dangers to reach a place where there were beasts that had a head like a pig's, a tail like a lion's, and two claws six feet broad with which they attacked our soldiers. Mingling with them were gryphons, which had beaks like an eagle's: they swooped down in our faces with great speed, but we defended ourselves against them with arrows and pikes. In that battle I lost 208 soldiers.

21 Next we came to a river, which flowed into the Ocean. The river was two and a half miles wide, and on its banks grew reeds so tall and broad that 30 soldiers could scarcely carry one of them. In that place there lived many elephants, but these, for I know not what reason, did us no harm. We built ships of the reeds and crossed the river to the other side. There we found men dressed in whaleskins. They gave us white sponges, purple shells and other sea shells, which held two or three gallons of liquid.[21] They also gave us tunics of sealskin and snail shells which held a pint of liquid. They placed before us worms which they had caught in the river, which were thicker than a man's thigh. They had a better savour than any other fish. They also gave us red mushrooms. They placed before us murries which weighed 250 pounds and said that there were even bigger ones in the Ocean, which was 23 miles away. They placed before us Sacred Fish[22] which weighed 150 pounds. In the same river there were women with long hair. When they saw strange men swimming in their river, they caught and drowned them, or dragged them among the reeds, where, because of their beauty, they either killed them in rage or forced them to have intercourse with them until they were dead. We caught two of these women: they were as white as snow and had long hair straggling down their backs.

22 We saw in the River Ganges many things which would seem marvellous were we to describe them. But I have decided not to write about anything which might seem incredible.

We went on to a castle inhabited by Indians, [and then to the Seres, who are said to be the most law-abiding of all peoples. They have no murder, adultery, perjury or drunkenness among them. They live on bread, vegetables and water. They led us by excellent routes through the Caspian Gates to Fasiace and to King Porus.] From there we followed the direction of the east wind until we came upon some wild beasts. They had bones projecting from the tops of their heads like sharp jagged swords. They struck many of our soldiers with these and pierced their shields. The soldiers killed as many as 8,450 of them. So, after many trials and dangers, we reached the kingdom of Porus. There I instructed one of my soldiers, Alcon by name, whom I had made ruler of Persia, to erect two statues of me in Babylon and in Persis. They were to be 25 feet high, of solid gold, and to have inscribed on them all my deeds. Alcon was to erect a further five golden statues of me, ten feet high, in furthest India, where there were a hundred statues in honour of Liber and Hercules.

Now, my dear teacher, I have made a memorandum of my remarkable deeds, which will be an object of amazement to succeeding generations; and I have established a new and durable record for heroic feats, which will both convey my fame to future ages and allow you, my master, to be acquainted with my care for you, my intelligence and my dedication.

The end of the letter of Alexander the Great, King of Macedon, to his master Aristotle.

2

On the Wonders of the East
[Letter of Pharasmanes to Hadrian]¹

[To the Emperor Hadrian. I have received your letter, Lord
Caesar, from Asacrates and Monacrates. When I read it I was
pleased to learn that you are well and in good spirits, and that
your empire has been expanded. In the meantime I have found
out about the nations of men and the nature of these parts, and
I send you a description appended to this letter. In addition I
report what I was able to learn from parents and relatives.

From the edge of Antioch it is 190 stades to the river Dirus;
this is a sacred place.]

1 The first city beyond Antimolima is 500 stades away, that is
368 leagues. This city has a great many sheep. 4. From there to
Babylon is 168 stades. This a great city of merchants, and there
are rams as big as oxen.

5 From there one comes to the city of the Medes called
Archemedon, which is as big as Babylon. It is 300 stades from
Babylon. 6. There are great monuments which were erected by
order of Alexander the Great. This land is 200 stades in length
and in breadth, or 133 miles and a half.

10 As you enter the Red Sea there is a place called Lentibelsinea,
where there are chickens like those among us, but of a red
colour. If anyone tries to catch one of them, the hand which
touched it is burnt up, and then his whole body. In addition
there are beasts here, which, when they hear the sound of a
man, they run away; they have eight feet, eyes like a gorgon's,
and two heads. If anyone wants to capture one, he goes armed.

11 Hascellentia is nine stades from Babylon, and lies at the foot
of the mountains of Media. It contains all kinds of good things.

Here there are serpents with two heads, whose eyes shine at night like lamps. There are also onagers with horns like oxen, very large.

12 Here on the right of Babylon they say is an unexplored region, on account of the serpents found there, which are called corsiae; they have horns like a ram's; if one of them bites you, you die. There is an abundance of pepper, which the serpents collect. The pepper is gathered in this way: they set fire to the places and the serpents escape underground. That is why pepper is black.

13 From Babylon to the Persian city where the pepper grows is 800 stades, or 620 miles and a half. The region is a desert because of the quantity of serpents.

14 Likewise there dwell there the Dog-heads, whom we call conopoenae: they have the manes of horses, the tusks of boars and the heads of dogs, and they breathe fire and flames.

15 Nearby is a wealthy city, full of good things.

16 From there one turns right towards Egypt. Hereabouts live men six feet tall, with beards down to their knees and hair down to their ankles. They are called homodubii [or Ichthyophagi] and they eat raw fish. There is also a river in that place called Gorgoneus [Gargarus]. There are found ants the size of dogs, with feet like locusts'. They are red and black and they dig for gold.[2] Whatever they dig up at night, they bring out about the fifth hour of the day. Men therefore take the risk of removing the gold; they carry it off on male camels and female ones with young; they leave the young tethered by the Gargulus and load the gold on to the female camels. They are drawn by mother-love to hurry back to their young, while the males stay where they are; so when the ants come in pursuit they find the male camels and eat them. While they are thus occupied, the females cross the river with the men. They go so fast you would think they were flying.

17 Between these two rivers – the Nile and the Brixontes [Brison] – there is a city called Locothea. The Nile is the chief of

rivers and flows through Egypt: the Egyptians call it Archobol-eta, i.e., Great Water. In this region there are a great many elephants. There are also men 15 feet tall with white bodies, a single head and two faces, red cheeks, a long nose and black hair. When the time for child-bearing comes they cross over in ships to India and give birth there. Again in Liconia in Gaul there are men of three colours with the heads of lions, 20 feet tall, and broad faces like winnowing fans. When they notice a man, or if anyone pursues them, they run away and sweat blood.

Across the Brixontes to the east there are tall, large men with legs 12 feet long, chest and abdomen seven feet long; they are black in colour and we call them hostes; anybody they capture, they eat.

There are also other beasts in the Brixontes called lertices, with asses' ears, a fleece like sheep and sheep's feet.

There is another island to the south of the Brixontes, where the men have no heads, but eyes and mouth in their chests: they are eight feet tall and about eight feet broad also. There are also serpents 150 feet long, as thick as columns. They are so numerous that no one can easily reach the lands across the river.

19 There is another region in the land of Babylon, where there is a huge mountain between Media and Armenia. Honest men dwell there; they include the Red Sea in their empire. There are precious stones there.

[20 On the right as you approach the Red Sea there are two cities named Phenix and Ioraba, where the men are very wealthy; from here are services to India and Arabia.]

21 Around this place there are women with beards down to their breasts, who wear horses' skins as clothing; they are great huntresses. Instead of hounds they rear tigers and leopards and all kinds of beasts which come from those parts, and they go hunting with them.

22 There are other women there who have tusks like a boar's, hair down to their ankles, and tails of oxen on their behinds. They are 13 feet tall, with beautiful bodies as white as marble,

and feet like those of a camel [and teeth like donkeys']. Many of them were killed because of their hideousness by Alexander the Great. Because he could not capture them alive, he killed them, because their bodies were shameless and unseemly.

23 Close to Ocean is a species of beasts called catani. They are very shapely, and [there are also men who] eat raw flesh and honey. To the left is the region of the catini, and the kings there are very hospitable, and rule over many lesser kings near the Ocean. On the left are many other kings. This race of men lives a long time. They are kindly men, and if anyone visits them, they send them back with some women. Alexander of Macedon, when he went there, was amazed by their humane qualities and had no wish to kill or harm them.

There are trees on which there grow precious stones.

24 There is another race of men, very black, who are known as Ethiopians.

Beyond this place there is another region, on the right of Ocean, 323 stades off, that is 256 leagues and one mile. Here live the Homodubii, who have the appearance of men down to their navels, but the rest of their body is like an onager's, with long feet like a bird's. Their voices are faint, and when they see men they run away.

25 To the borders of Ocean is 380 stades. In that place there are the Soraci, who are called Tritognides among us: they are like gods, and they can give you an answer to any question you ask them.

26 There is another place full of savage men. There are 110 kings and they are very savage. There are also two places, one of the Sun and the other of the Moon. The place of the Sun is warm by day and cold by night, and the place of the Moon is cold by day and warm by night. They are both 200 stades long (133 leagues and half a mile). In this place there grow trees resembling the laurel and the olive: balsam is found in these trees. From here you go on to another place 151 stades off (50 leagues and one mile).

There is an island in the Red Sea where dwells a race of men whom we call Donestre; they are semi-divine. They are like men down to their navels, and the rest of their body is [not] human in appearance; they speak the language of the nations. When they see men of another race, they address them in their own language, using the names of their parents and relations, charming them with their conversation; thus deceiving them, they destroy them. When they have captured them, they kill and eat them; afterwards they take the head of the man they have eaten, and lament over it.

Further east are men 15 feet tall and ten feet broad, with big heads and ears like winnowing fans; they use one as a mattress at night, and with the other they cover themselves over. Their bodies are delicate and white as milk. When they see men, they lift their ears and run a long way off, so fast you would think they were flying.

There is another island where there are men whose eyes shine like lamps.

27 There is another island 360 stades long and broad (110 leagues), where there is a temple of Bel, built in the days of King Iobis. It is of bronze and iron and is called Beliobilis [Heliopolis]. To the east is a temple of the Sun, where there is a silent priest, who watches over the maritime towns.

There is a golden vine in the east, near the Sun's rising, which is 150 feet long and bears gems like grapes. [Under the vine] there is an ivory couch 260 feet long.

28 There is a mountain called Adamant, where the gryphon bird is found: it has four feet, the head of an eagle and the tail of an ox. In the same mountain is the bird called Phoenix, which has a crest like a peacock's tail; it builds its nest from cinnamon. Every thousand years it kindles a fire in its own nest and is reborn from its ashes.

There is another mountain where there are black men, whom no one can come near, because the mountain is on fire.

3

Excerpt from 'The Chronicle of George the Monk' (I.19)

ALEXANDER OF MACEDON

After Philip, Alexander his son was King of Macedonia. In his time Darius the son of Arsames was ruler of all his empire in succession to Chous. In the fourth year of his reign God sent Alexander, the King of Macedonia, against the Assyrians, Persians, Medes and Parthians. Alexander took arms against Darius the King of the Persians and went to the city of Byzas in Europe,[1] where he founded a city, in which he gathered his army and called it Strategis. From there he advanced a little and made a distribution of gold to his people, and called the place Chrysopolis. He shot forward like a panther with a great strength against the lands and cities of the east. He captured Tyre and sent ambassadors to Judaea to ask them for an alliance against Persia. But they were afraid of Darius because of their inferiority and would not receive the ambassadors, and they made a treaty not to fight against him. At this Alexander was angry and attacked Judaea. The High Priest Jaddua, following a divine revelation, put on his priestly garb and went out to meet Alexander, and to dazzle him and win him over.[2]

The High Priest was dressed in the old fashion, as follows. His robe reached from his head to his feet, and was encrusted with gold; he wore a belt of purple and white linen, adorned and decorated with gold and aquamarines. On the edges he had embroidered tassels shaped like pomegranates, composed of twisted strands of blue, red and purple linen: attached to the middle of these tassels were bells of pure gold, hanging down all round the fringes of the garment. He also wore a tunic of linen, embroidered in red, blue, purple and gold and all kinds of colours; it reached his thighs and was secured with a belt similar to the first, which is referred to as the scapulary or ephod. This garment is also called Akylas, and is fastened on either shoulder with brooches of sardonyx set in fine gold, and in addition another dozen gems of exceptional size and beauty, quite heavy to carry, which were arranged in rows on either side, likewise set in gold and having three stones in each row – a marvellous sight to behold. The first row contained a sardonyx, a chrysolite and an emerald, the second a garnet, a jasper and a sapphire, the third a brilliant, an amethyst and an agate, and the fourth a topaz, an onyx and a beryl. On all these the names of the patriarchs were inscribed, each stone bearing the names of one of the twelve tribes.

Along with the ephod in the middle of the chest was a square piece of material one span long and one span wide, decorated in the same way as the ephod, which in Hebrew is also called ephod or phoessin, but in Greek is referred to as the revealer, by means of which God foretells victory to those who are going to war. There was such a gleam from the stones on it, even before the army had begun to move, and especially from the diamond which gave the oracles, that the assembled multitude thought that God himself was present to help them. In the centre he had something like a star, all of gold, with emeralds on either side in rows of six, inscribed with the twelve tribes of Israel, and between the two emeralds a diamond.

When the High Priest wants to question God, he fixes on the scapulary in the middle of his chest and places his hands underneath it, enfolding it in his palms as if in a box. Then Saul, wanting the priest quickly to prepare for war, instructs him, 'Bring your hands together and raise up the ephod.' So then he looks at the ephod and asks God his question, directly and clearly to the diamond, which changes colour by divine power and by its changes indicates to the people what is to be. If it turns black it means death, if red, slaughter, if white the favour of God.

In addition there were letters of pure bronze, one for each letter of the Hebrew alphabet, which the priest would bring before the Lord, placing them on his ephod and asking his question: immediately the letters would rise up through the power of God and make clear whether God was for or against. So, if the matter about which inquiry was made was according to God's will, only those rose up which indicated Yes, but if against his will, only those which indicated No. Yes, and so it was with all other questions to the Lord, if they were in favour with Him; but if He was angry at them, He would make no reply through these indicators nor through any other divine revelations and prophecies.

Thus he says: Saul has seen the invasion of the foreigners and is afraid, and his heart has leapt mightily, and he has inquired of the Lord, and the Lord has not answered him by dreams or signs or prophecies; he has made no reply at all. Then Saul said to his children, 'Fetch me a woman who gives oracles from her belly.'

On his head he wore a kind of gold-plated belt like what is called a diadem or tiara, in which a leaf of gold hung down over his forehead, on which the name of God was written in gold letters, just as he revealed the divine name when he said to Moses 'I am that I am.' This is not to be spoken among the Hebrews, and it is forbidden to them to utter it; but it is written with four letters, so that it is known as the tetragram; and the Samaritans call it Iabe, but the Jews Aeia. The fourfold colour of the priestly dress is a symbol of these four letters, from which all things were made. The High Priest puts these on mystically and reverently and goes into the sanctuary and prays to the creator and lord of the universe on their behalf. The linen represents the earth, the aquamarine the air, the purple the water and the red colour fire. These comprise all that can be perceived or conceived. The tabernacle is covered with gold both inside and outside, with a roof of woven cloths of many colours. One was purple, one red or rose, one blue as aquamarine, and the linen pure white. These were, as stated above, riddling allusions to the four elements. The aquamarine is like the air, the red or rose like fire, the purple represents the sea (for the sea gives birth to the murex shell from which the purple dye is made), and the linen the earth, for that is what it grows from. God has thus placed the entire universe on the shoulders of the High Priest to amaze the people with the splendour of his dress, and to teach the priests themselves that they must adorn their souls and place on them the adornment of virtue.

So when the High Priest, with all the other priests and the assembled people, had made themselves conspicuous in these glorious vestments, they stood in a prominent place, where there was a fine view of the temple, to meet the conqueror. When Alexander saw the crowd in the distance in their white clothing, and the priests in their linen garb, so grave and splendid, and the High Priest in blue and gold with his tiara and the golden plate on it, on which the name of God was inscribed, as I explained, he was amazed at the unusual sight; he immediately dismounted from his chariot, came forward and bowed down before the name of God and greeted the High Priest; then all the Jews with one voice cried out and welcomed him, as did the priests.

The kings of Syria and all the others were amazed and thought that Alexander had taken leave of his senses. Parmenion his general was particularly amazed and angry at his making obeisance like one of his subjects. But Alexander explained: 'I was not making obeisance to the High Priest but to the god whom he honours and who has promised me help against my enemies. For when I was planning my expedition against Persia, and was daunted by the size of his empire, the god appeared to me in a dream dressed like this High Priest and told me to take courage and reach after my ambition. He in fact said to me, "I will knock down the dynasty of Persia to you." So when I saw him dressed like this I remembered my dream and made obeisance to him.'

Thereupon he introduced Parmenion to the High Priest and, accompanied by the other priests, he entered the city of Jerusalem and was received with great joy by the Jews. The scribes brought out the Book of Daniel and explained to him the prophecy the prophet had pronounced, that it was fated that one of the Macedonians would conquer the empire of Persia.[3]

Alexander was pleased and delighted at this; he went up to the temple and sacrificed to God according to the High Priest's directions. He paid due honours to the High Priest and all the other priests, and decorated the temple with large and lavish dedications. Then he set off for Persia.

He took some of the Jews as his allies; pre-eminent among them was a man named Mosomachos,[4] a noble soul and an excellent archer. While they were on the march towards Babylon, one of the seers stopped the army to take omens from the flight of birds. Mosomachos asked why the column had halted, and the seer replied with his interpretation of the omen: 'If it remains unmoved, it will be best for everyone to halt, but if it rises and flies on ahead, we should march forward, while if it flies backward, we should retreat.' When Mosomachos heard this he surreptitiously drew his bow and shot the bird. The seer was very angry, as were those who were compelled to take part in the march. He took the dead bird in his hands and said: 'Why do you blame me, you poor devils? Surely this bird, recognising his own salvation, has made plain to you what is to your advantage? If it had been able to know the future, it would not have come to this place, for fear of being shot by Mosomachos.' When he said this they were all ashamed.

So Alexander drew up his army against Darius at Isopolis[5] in Cilicia. He defeated him, slaughtered many of his army and captured the entire kingdom, including the lands of the Medes, the Persians, the Parthians and the Babylonians, and in addition all the parts of India and its kingdoms except for the kingdom of Candace,[6] the widowed ruler of inner India, who took him prisoner in the following way.

It was Alexander's custom, when he sent ambassadors to enemy rulers, to accompany them disguised as a common soldier, and to see what the ruler was like. Candace had learnt of this and contrived to find out what his appearance was and what were his distinguishing marks. Learning that he was small, with big prominent teeth and one grey eye and one black one, she made a note of this for herself. So when he came to her with his ambassadors she recognised him from these features, and took hold of him, saying: 'King Alexander, you have captured the whole world, but a woman has taken you captive.' He replied: 'Because of your cunning and devious intelligence, I will leave you and your sons and your kingdom unharmed, and I will take you to be my wife.' So he took her with him to Egypt, where he founded the great city of Alexandria, and then returned to Babylon, where he died at the age of 32, after a reign of twelve years.

He built many monuments, so magnificent that they defy description. For this reason the prophet described him as a winged leopard, for his immense speed and energy, and the fact that he flew through the world, marking his path with victories and trophies. It is said that he heard one of the philosophers proclaim that there are infinite worlds. At this he groaned loudly: 'If there are many worlds, I have not conquered even one completely.'[7] So great was he in his conceptions, his ambition and his nobility. He became known and admired everywhere for his wisdom and understanding, his quick intelligence and his philosophy. As a pupil of Aristotle, he had had a thorough training in logic. He was very warlike and brave. Once, when he saw a namesake of his fighting like a coward, he said to him: 'Change your ways, or else your name.' So the wisdom with which he was adorned became more conspicuous as a result of his victories. When he took prisoner the daughters of Darius, who were renowned for their beauty, he did not presume even to look at them, for he said it would be shameful and unusual, and even ridiculous, for a man who had defeated men with his bravery to be conquered by women.

He reached the furthest parts of India and the great Ocean which encircles the world, and in it the great island of the Brahmans. He discovered their wonderful, even superhuman, way of life, their reverence and worship of the God of all things, by which he was very impressed, admiring the heights of philosophy which these men had reached. He set up a pillar in that place with the following inscription: 'I, Alexander the Great, reached this place.'[8]

In that island live the so-called Long-lived Ones.[9] Most of them live to the age of 150 because of the pure and well-balanced atmosphere and the undiscoverable judgement of God. In that place every kind of fruit is in season all year round, inasmuch as while one is in flower, another is ripening and another is ready to harvest. The large Indian nuts grow there, and the spices which we love so much and which are so hard to obtain, and the stone called magnet. The people of the Brahmans are very pious and they live a life without possessions, a destiny allotted to them by the judgement of God. They dwell by a river, living naked according to nature and constantly praising God. They have no animals, they do not farm, they use no iron, no houses, no fire, no gold or silver, no bread or wine, they wear no clothes and eat no meat, and engage in none of the things that require work or result in pleasure; they use the moist, sweet, well-blended and beautiful air to fend off all kinds of sickness or disease; they enjoy a little fruit and pure water, all the while honouring and praising God unceasingly.

The men live on the side of the river towards Ocean, and the women on this side of the river Ganges (which flows into Ocean in the region of India). The men cross over to the women in the months of July and August, which are the cool ones with them, as the sun tilts towards us and the north: at this time their bodies are supposed to be best disposed for intercourse. That is also, apparently, the reason why the Nile does not flood at the same time as other rivers, but inundates Egypt in high summer, because the sun is running its course through the northern regions and, at the time when it shrinks and obstructs all other rivers, it is at its furthest from this one. After spending 40 days with their women they cross over again. After a woman has borne two children her husband does not cross over to her again, while she takes good care not to approach any other man. If any of the women should turn out to be infertile, and fails to bear a child after five annual crossings by her husband, he does not approach her again. As a result, the population of the land is not very numerous, because of their continence and contentment with little. Such is the way of life of the Brahmans.

They say that the river is very difficult to cross because of the so-called Odontotyrannus.[10] This is a huge amphibious beast which lives in the river and is big enough to swallow an elephant whole. But during the 40 days when the men are making their crossing, it disappears by the dispensation of God. In addition there are giant snakes in the deserts, 70 cubits long and very thick. They are extremely frightening, and display conspicuously the wisdom and glory of the Creator. There are also scorpions a cubit long, and ants as long as the palm of the hand. As a result these deserts are difficult to cross, and are uninhabited because of the fearsome venomous beasts. There are a great many elephants in those places, which go about grazing in herds.

In fact the great Caesarius,[11] brother of Gregory the Great, in his description of various races and their laws and customs, writes as follows (I summarise): 'In every land and in every nation there is either a written law-code or customary usage. Law teaches ancestral lore to the lawless. First among these are the Seres, who live on the edge of the earth: they have a written law incorporating ancestral custom, which forbids adultery and traffic with prostitutes, theft, slander, murder and every sort of crime.

'There is a law also among the Bactrians or Brahmans and Islanders; it consists of an education and religious practice focused on the ancestors, and forbids the eating of meat, the drinking of wine, lechery and all other kinds of evil, the sanction being their fear of and trust in God. Yet the Indians next door engage in foul murder, wine-bibbing and all kinds of wild excess in shameful behaviour, and in the even remoter parts they eat people, particularly picking on strangers who come to them, and tearing them apart like dogs.

'The Chaldaeans and Babylonians have different customs again, involving marrying their mothers, sibling infanticide, murder and all practices hateful to God: they regard these things as virtuous, even if they are far from their own country.

'Among the Gauls it is customary for the women to work the fields, build houses, and do all kinds of men's work, and also to prostitute themselves to whomever they like, without any objection or envy from their husbands. Some of these women are very warlike and will hunt animals, at least those that are not too fierce. They are rulers of their households and dominate their husbands.

'In Britain many men sleep with a single woman, and many women with a single man, and they regard what is immoral as moral and ancestral custom, and do so without arousing objection or envy.

'The Amazons have no husbands, but like wild animals they cross their borders once a year, at the spring equinox, and have intercourse with the neighbouring men, making a kind of huge party and festival out of it. Then when they have conceived they all go home again. When they give birth, they kill all the male children, but preserve the female ones and nurse them with every attention until they grow up.'

After the death of Alexander his kingdom was divided into many dominions . . .

4
Palladius, 'On the
Life of the Brahmans'

I

1 Your disposition to hard work and study, your love of what is fine and your love of God (the adornment of noble men) has encouraged me once again to discourse to you on a subject abundantly filled with philosophic interest. Trusting myself to your eagerness to listen, I shall outline to you, in addition to the previous topic, the life of the Brahmans. I have not myself explored their country or met any of their people. They live far away from us on the borders of India and China, on the banks of the Ganges. I myself have only visited the near extremities of India: I was there a few years ago with the blessed Moses, Bishop of Adule, but I could not endure the summer heat and was seized by a severe fever – the water there being such that it bubbles up out of the spring in an excessively cold state and has to be boiled at once in buckets – so that having seen only so much I came home again. This river Ganges is the one that we call Phison, which is mentioned in the Scriptures as one of the four rivers that flow out of Paradise.[1]

2 There is a story that Alexander, the King of Macedon, investigated the life of the Brahmans; but he was quickly satisfied with hearsay. Even he, I believe, did not cross the Ganges, but penetrated as far as the borders of Serica (where the silk worms [*seres*] produce the silk), and erected a stone pillar with this inscription: 'Alexander the King of Macedon reached this place.'[2]

3 I have learnt what I know about the Brahmans from a certain Theban scholar, who made his journey of his own free will, but

against his will was taken into captivity. According to his own report, he made a bad job of his defence and, not caring where he went, conceived a desire to study the land of the Indians.

4 He sailed with an older man first to Adule and then to Axum,[3] where the petty king of the Indians had his seat. He spent some time there and became well acquainted with the king; then he wanted to go to the island of Taprobane,[4] where the so-called Long-livers dwell. In fact these people live on that island for as long as 150 years; they achieve this remarkable age thanks to the excellence of the climate and the unfathomable judgement of God. The great king of the Indians lives on this island: all the petty kings are subject to him, like satraps, as the scholar explained to me – though he had the information from others, since he himself was not able to go to the island.

5 If the report is true, there are about a thousand other islands close by that island, all encircled by the Red Sea.[5] Now in those islands, which are called the Manioloi, is found the stone called magnet which draws iron to it. If anyone tries to leave the islands in a ship which has iron rivets, it is held fast by the power of the stone, and cannot sail away. Naturally enough, for this reason all the ships that ply to the great island are joined together with wooden pegs and without iron.

6 There are, he said, five very large rivers in that island, which are navigable by ships. According to what they told him, the season of fruitfulness never ceases in that place: at any one time one branch is in fruit, another is being reaped, another is still ripening. Dates grow there, and the large Indian nut. The dwellers in the place live on milk and rice, and as they do not have wool or flax they gird their loins with finely worked skins of animals. The sheep have long hair but not wool, they give plenty of milk and have fat tails. The people are accustomed to eat the meat of goats and sheep; the pig is not found in India or Ethiopia, because of the heat, except in Thebes.

7 This scholar told me: 'I found some Indians from Axum crossing over in ships for the purpose of trade, and tried to cross

over among them. We came close to the Bedsades, where the pepper comes from' – they are a small, feeble people, who live in caves in the rocks and are good at climbing on the tumbled heaps of rocks;[6] they go about to collect pepper from the pepper trees. These are stunted little shrubs, according to the scholar. The Bedsades are also stunted little men with big heads and unshaven straggly hair, while the rest of the Ethiopians and Indians are black and stalwart and fuzzy-haired.

8 'I was conducted from there by the ruler and brought to trial for attempting to enter their land. They would not accept my defence, as they did not understand the language of our country, neither did I know what laws they claimed that I had infringed. I did not understand their language, and we only managed to communicate with each other by expressive grimaces. I guessed that they were making accusations against me from the blood-shot appearance of their eyes and the wild gnashing of their teeth, and from the vehemence of their voices. They for their part, guided by my trembling and struggling, and my paleness, were able to deduce from the fearful aspect of my body the misery of my soul.

9 'Well, I was held by them for a period of six years, during which I was put to work in a bakery. The king's regular consumption of grain was a single modius [two gallons] for the whole palace, but I have no idea where he got it from. And so, in the course of the six years I learnt to use their language quite well, and discovered a good deal about the neighbouring peoples.

10 'I obtained my release in the following way. Another king was making war with the one who held me prisoner, and he informed on him to the great king, the one who has his seat in the island of Taprobane: he told the great king that this king was holding a distinguished Roman prisoner and forcing him to ignominious labour. The great king then sent one of his judges to investigate, and on discovering the truth ordered him to be flayed alive for abusing a Roman citizen. They are, you see, very

afraid and respectful of the power of Rome, believing that Rome could easily conquer their country because of its superior strength in men and engines of war.'

11 So this man told me that the Brahmans are a race set apart, not by choice,[7] but by the dispensation of God above, who has appointed them to live according to nature, in nakedness, on the banks of the river.[8] They keep no four-footed animals, and use no farmland, no iron, no houses, no fire, no bread, no wine, no clothing, nor any of the other things that are designed for use or enjoyment. They make use of the purest, finest and most wholesome air. They reverence God and have some slight knowledge of him, and although they are unable to analyse the ways of Providence in a sophisticated manner, they nevertheless pray unceasingly. When they pray they gaze earnestly at the sky rather than in the direction of the east, and they do not trouble to face east at all.

12 They eat whatever fresh green shoots and wild herbs they find – whatever the ground brings forth of its own accord. They drink water, and live a wandering life in the forests, taking their rest upon beds of leaves. They have an abundance of persea wood and the so-called thorny plants, and various other local seed-bearing plants, which they live on.

13 Their men live on the far side of the Ganges in the quarter towards Ocean. (The Ganges in fact flows into Ocean.) Their women, however, live on this side of the Ganges, in the Indian sector. The men cross over to the women in the months of July and August, which are the cold months among them, when the sun gains height towards the north and comes closer to us;[9] these months are regarded as more temperate by them, and conducive to the sexual urge. After 40 days' intercourse with the women they cross back again. When a woman has given birth to two children, her husband does not cross over again to enjoy his wife's company, but sends a substitute and practises continence thenceforth. If one of the women should chance to be found barren, her husband will keep on crossing over for a

period of five years to have intercourse with her; but if she still does not conceive, he does not approach her again. As a result, that race is not very numerous, because of the hard conditions of life in the place and because of their natural self-restraint in procreation.

14 Such is the way of life of the Brahmans. The river is supposed to be very hard to cross, because of the so-called Odontotyrannus.[10] This is a really enormous creature which lives in the river, and is able to swallow an entire elephant and a man all at once. At the time when the Brahmans cross over to visit their wives it does not frequent the area. There are also very large serpents around the rivers, up to a hundred feet long; I have seen the skin of one which was more than two feet broad. The ants there are a palm long, and the scorpions up to 18 inches. As a result it is very unsafe to travel through the region. Not every spot in that region has so many beasts and poisonous creatures; they are found mainly in the uninhabited areas. There are also many herds of elephants.

15 I am sending you, with this explanatory note, a little work I have acquired by Arrian,[11] the student of the philosopher Epictetus[12] – the one who was made a slave because of his handsome appearance and turned to philosophy in the reign of the Emperor Nero, who put to death the apostles Peter and Paul – and historian of Alexander. If you read it with attention and ponder on it, you will live the better.

II

1 [Dandamis, the teacher of the Brahmans, described their way of life as follows:]

'King Alexander, not content to be king only of Macedonia, and not satisfied with Philip for a father, claimed to be the son of Ammon as well; he spread abroad a false account of his birth and pursued an invincible career as a warrior. He rose like the sun in Macedon, and rode across the whole world before setting in Babylon; he regarded Europe and Asia as too confined for him, and came to examine and investigate our part of the world also.'

2 When he came, Alexander prayed inwardly as follows: 'O Wisdom, mother of Providence,[13] who holds the power of all virtues in your hands, enthroned above with truth alone, nurse and creator of nature, giver of reason, observer of all knowledge, who art far removed from injustice but art gentle with the just, grant me kindly the achievement of my desires. I have come here to see the wise and good Brahmans, after hearing about them from one of them, Calanus, who came to join me. Persuaded by him, I have come eagerly to see and to learn.'

3 The Brahmans and the Indians spoke to Alexander as follows.
'You have come to us Brahmans in search of wisdom, which we were the first to receive and which is the ruling principle in our lives. This is what you wanted to learn, King Alexander. The philosopher is not a subject but a ruler, no man has power over him. But since, up until now, you have traduced and mistrusted us, you may now have a taste of true discourse.

4 'Calanus[14] was, as far as we are concerned, a wicked man, and it is through Calanus that you Greeks came to know about the Brahmans. He was not one of us, but could not be dissuaded from running after riches. It was not good enough for him to drink the water of self-control from the River Tiberoboam[15] and to feed on fresh milk, by which the mind is made more like the divine. He had wealth, the enemy of the soul, and terrible fire blazed within him, turning him away from wisdom towards pleasure. None of us rolls on red hot coals, and no pain wastes our bodies; our way of life is the recipe for our health.

5 'We are by nature without riches, and death is as much our companion as life. If any mortal men, instructed by lying tales, aim their vacuous darts at us, they do no damage to our freedom. To be deceived is the same as to be quickly convinced; the deceiver wrongs the one whom he persuades, and the persuaded does wrong in holding to his deceiver before he has

learnt the truth. Calumny is the mother of war and produces the rage which engenders wars and battles.

6 'There is no manliness in killing men; it is the action of a bandit. True manliness consists in fighting the changes of climate with the naked body, removing the lusts of the belly and conquering the warfare within, rather than being overcome by desire and the search for glory, wealth and pleasure. These, Alexander, are what you must first conquer, these you must kill. If you conquer these, you will have no need to fight against external foes. The purpose of fighting external foes is only to bring tribute to these internal desires. Do you not see that you conquer your external foes but are conquered by the internal ones? How many kings of foolishness do you think rule over fools? Sight, hearing, smell, taste, touch, tongue, stomach, genitals, the entire flesh of your body. There are many of them within, like implacable mistresses and insatiable tyrants, making endless demands; desires, avarice, love of pleasure, murder, assassination, meanness, dispute: to all of these and more men are enslaved, for these they kill and are killed.

7 'The Brahmans have won this inner warfare and have recovered; now we take our ease, contemplating matter and the heavens. We listen to the sweet song of the birds and the clangour of eagles. We are clothed in leaves and live in the open air. We eat fruit and drink water. We sing hymns to God and look forward to the future. We listen to no one who is of no advantage to us. We avoid much speech and practise silence. That is how we Brahmans live.

8 'You speak of what is to be done, and do what should not be spoken of; none of you considers a man a philosopher unless he talks a lot; your mind is your tongue and your brains are in your lips. You collect gold and silver, you need slaves and large houses, you pursue power, you eat and drink as much as the beasts, and you are unaware of yourselves. You dress yourselves in soft clothing like silkworms. You do practically anything and then regret it. You speak of yourselves as of enemies; though

you have power over your tongues you are at war with them. Those who are silent are better than you, since they do not practise self-accusation.

9 'You shear the fleeces of sheep. You glory in what encircles your fingers, like those of prisoners, as if the rings were idols. You wear gold like women and take pride in it. Playing the Creator, you fashion and encourage a temper like that of wild beasts. You surround yourselves with many possessions and take pride in them, blind to the fact that none of them can help you to the truth: gold does not sustain the soul, nor fatten the body; quite the contrary, it darkens the soul and emaciates the body.

10 'We, however, seeking to discover through nature the truth, take thought for whatever she allots. When we are hungry, we feast on fresh shoots and vegetables, which have been carefully arranged for us by Providence. When we are thirsty, we go to the river; trampling on gold, we drink water and thus allay our thirst. Gold does not quench thirst, nor allay hunger;[16] it does not heal wounds or cure diseases, nor does it satiate greed, but rather aggravates this desire which is alien to nature. For it is plain that when a man is thirsty he desires to drink water, and when he has done so his thirst is over; and that when a man is hungry he seeks food and when he has eaten he is satisfied, and ceases from his desire. Every human desire ceases when it is satisfied, because this is inherent in nature. But the desire for wealth knows no satiety, because it is against nature. That is why you adorn yourselves with it and glory in it, regarding yourselves as superior to other men. And that is why you take as your own what belongs to everyone: avarice divides up the single nature which is common to all into a multitude of portions.

11 'Calanus, our false friend, was of this mind, but he is despised by us; responsible as he is for many evils, he is honoured and held in great regard by you; but we sent him away as being worthless to us, and of no account. Calanus, that

greedy and vain man, that friend of yours, was wild about all those things we do not pursue; he is no friend of ours. Useless and more miserable than the wretched of the earth, he lost his soul through his avarice. For that reason we regarded him as unworthy of us, and unworthy of the friendship of God, of our freedom and our lack of disturbance.[17] He could not relax and luxuriate in the pleasures of the forest, and he had no hope for what is to come, for he had murdered his own poor soul with avarice.

12 'There is a man among us named Dandamis, who lies in the woods on fresh leaves, keeping close by a spring as if suckling on the pure milk of a mother.'

13 When King Alexander heard this he summoned their teacher and leader, wishing to hear him talk. But they showed him where Dandamis was. Alexander went there but could not see him, as he was lying among the woods, resting peacefully on leaves, close by a spring from which he drank as if milking the breast of mother earth. When Alexander could not see Dandamis, the commander and teacher of the Brahmans, he sent to him a friend of his, Onesicratus[18] by name, with the following orders:

14 'Go quickly, Onesicratus, to the teacher of the Brahmans. Either bring the man to me or find out where he is so that I can go to him myself.'

'I will do as you say at once', replied Onesicratus. 'It is yours to command, mine to perform.'

Then he went to the great man Dandamis, found him and said:

'Greetings, teacher of the Brahmans. The son of mighty Zeus, King Alexander, who is the lord of all men, summons you. If you come to him he will give you many fine gifts; but if you do not come he will cut off your head.'

When Dandamis heard that, he smiled kindly. He did not raise his head from the leaves, but laughed at the man and replied as follows from his lying position:

15 'God, the great king, is the source of no violence, but of light, peace, life, water, and of the human body and soul; and he receives the souls that have not been conquered by desire, when fate releases them. This is my only lord and god, who sets his face against murder and does not take part in warfare. Alexander is no god, for he knows that he must die. How can he be lord of all men, when he has not yet crossed the Tiberoboam or the Cossoalus, when he has not set up his throne in Palibothra,[19] when he has not passed Zonenades, nor seen the course of the sun either in Mesopotamia, or in the Borderlands or the Karisoborioi. Scythia has not yet learnt his name. If the land over there is not enough for him, let him cross the Ganges and he will find a land capable of bearing men, if the land over there is no longer able to hold him.

16 'As for Alexander's promises to me and the presents he says he will give me, they are useless to me. The following things are what is dear and valuable and useful to me: my home, these leaves, and my nourishment, these plants on the shore, and water to drink. All other goods and wealth are assembled with trouble (and those who assemble them perish with them) and provide nothing but grief, with which every mortal is filled. But now I sleep on a bed of leaves, with my eyes closed, seeing nothing: if I should desire to look at gold I should disturb my rest. The earth provides everything for me, as a mother provides milk for her child. What I need, I can go for; what I do not want, no one can force me to worry about.

17 'If Alexander takes away my head he will not destroy my soul, but only my head which will fall silent. My soul will depart to my lord, leaving my body like an old garment on the earth, from which it was taken. I shall become breath and ascend to my lord, who enclosed us in flesh when he placed us on earth, in order to try us and find out whether we would live according to his commandments. When we depart to him he will ask us for an account and will act as judge of all our violent actions. The groans of the wronged will be the punishment of the wrongdoers.[20]

18 'Let Alexander make his threats to those who desire gold and fear death; against us, these two weapons are useless. The Brahmans do not love gold, nor fear death. Go and say to Alexander: "Dandamis does not need what you have. Therefore he will not come to you. If you need Dandamis, you must come to him."'

19 When Alexander received this report from Onesicratus, he was even more keen to see Dandamis, saying that he who had conquered so many peoples had been conquered by one naked old man. So he went with 15 friends to Dandamis' forest. As he approached him, he dismounted from his horse and took off his crown and all his other motley. He went alone into the wood to the place where Dandamis was and greeted him as follows:

'Greetings Dandamis, teacher of the Brahmans, lord of wisdom. I heard your name and have come to see you, since you will not come to see me.'

'Greetings to you', Dandamis replied, 'who have overthrown so many cities and displaced so many peoples.'

20 Alexander sat down at his feet for that hour, in a piece of land that was free from the taint of blood.

'Why have you come to see us?' Dandamis asked. 'What do you want to carry off from our solitude? We do not have what you are looking for; and you do not desire what we have. We honour God, love men, have no care for wealth, despise death, take no thought of pleasure; but you fear death, love gold, seek pleasure, hate men and despise God.'

'I have come to learn wisdom from you', replied Alexander. 'They say that you are like a god. I want to know how you are different from the Greeks, and if you can see or understand more than other men.'

21 'I would like to offer you some account of the wisdom of God', responded Dandamis, 'and to instil in you a god-fearing mind. But you have no room in your soul to accommodate the gift of God that I can offer you. Your soul is full of unfulfilled desires, insatiable avarice and superstitious love of power, which

make it hard for me to draw you here and stop you slaughtering peoples and pouring out the blood of nations. It seems to me that your companions will be sorry if they see a city remaining intact and its people saved. You say that you are going to the Ocean[21] and beyond that to the rest of the world, and after that to another one; and you will be very sorry if you do not keep what you conquer. How then can I talk to you of the wisdom of God, when your mind is so full of this nonsense and these unfulfilled desires, which not even the submission of the entire universe could satisfy?

22 'You were created small of stature and naked, and came into the world alone: what is it that makes you great enough to slaughter all these people? To seize all their possessions? When you have conquered everybody, and taken possession of all the world, you will possess no more land than I have as I lie down.[22] We control just as much land as we were made from, and we, whom you so despise, possess as much without wars and battles as you do: earth, water and air. Everything I have, I hold justly, and I desire nothing; but you, however much you make war and shed blood and slaughter people, and even if you conquer all the rivers in the world, will drink no more water than I do. I do not fight, or bear wounds, or raze cities, and I have as much earth and water as you.

23 'Learn this piece of wisdom from me, Alexander: desire nothing, and everything will be yours, and you will lack nothing. Desire is the mother of penury; penury is the result of indiscipline treated with bad medicines. It is miserable because it never finds what it seeks, is never content with what it has, but is tortured with lust for what it does not have.

24 'You can enjoy a pleasant wealth like mine if you will come and live with me; if you will listen and attend to my teaching, you will acquire good things from me. God is my companion, and is alive within me. I do not listen to evil men. The sky is my roof, the earth my bed, the woods my table, fruit my food, rivers my cup-bearers. I do not eat flesh like a lion, the flesh of other

animals does not rot within me, I do not become a grave of dead animals. Providence gives me fruit for food, as a mother gives milk to her child.

25 'Now, you wish to learn from me, Alexander, what I have that is more than other men, and how my wisdom is superior to theirs. As you see, I live as I was created in the beginning. I live naked as I was born from my mother, without wealth or care. For this reason I know what God does and understand what is to come. You marvel when you read oracles of what is to come to you day by day, while you do not understand the works of God which are demonstrated to you every hour – plagues, famines, wars, thunderstorms, droughts, rain and blight. All these I foreknow. Providence also gives me knowledge of how, whence and why these occur. This gives me exceeding pleasure, that God has made me his fellow-counsellor in his works and shown such justice to me. If fear of war or some other calamity troubles a king, he comes to me, as to a messenger of God, and I, interceding with the Providence of God, persuade her to do something good for my visitor.[23] Thus I dispel his fear and send him away encouraged.

26 'Tell me, which is better – to harm men and have a bad reputation, or to protect them and be known as a benefactor? What is more fitting to the sons of God – to fight and tear down what has been created by Providence, or to live at peace and to reconstruct what has been damaged and thrown down, as a servant of Providence? This power of yours, Alexander, will not help you, nor your abundance of gold, your herds of elephants, your variety of beautiful clothing which you wear, your army which now follows in your footsteps, your horses and pikemen and all the other things you have plundered from others in war and battle. But you will derive great benefit if you take my advice and listen to my teaching.

27 'I am not frightened of your killing me, Alexander, if I tell you what you need to hear. I shall simply depart to my God who created all things. He knows that I am just, and nothing is

hidden from him, whose eyes are the stars, moon and sun, and he judges the wrongdoers. You cannot avoid his eye, and there is no place where you can flee from him, or avoid his justice. Do not throw down what God wishes to create, do not annihilate by force what he wishes to set in order, do not shed the blood of cities, do not march on the corpses of nations. It is more important for you to live than to kill others, and to avoid death and bless others, and to know that it is a punishment, not a gain, to seize the goods of others.

28 'Why do you, who have but a single soul, want to destroy so many nations? Why do you, who take your joy in your own foolishness, fill the world with so much misery? Why do you regard other people's misfortunes as gain to yourself? Why do you laugh at people weeping? Think of me, naked and poor in the wilderness, and benefit yourself; stop your wars and bid welcome to Peace, the beloved of Providence. Do not seek to display your valour in the midst of wickedness, but spend your life in tranquillity with us. Throw away your fleeces, torn from sheep, and do not rely on corpses for covering. You will honour yourself by imitating us, for you will become as you were when you were created. In the wilderness, the soul is tempted towards virtue.

29 'Make your choice, King Alexander, and lead a life with us, free of material things. Perhaps you will be fortunate enough, as you follow our teaching, to discover yourself. Now, the Macedonians lead you on so that they can overthrow cities, kill men and seize their goods, and the shedders of foreign blood are unhappy if they see a nation survive. They are soldiers for their own greed, using your leadership as an unjust excuse.

30 'When will you embark on the life without care that was allotted to you by God, and live for yourself rather than killing others? Now that you have heard my words, what sort of future do you plan for yourself? Will you choose to scale the heights, disturb the nations and kill men? What you have done is one thing, but what you do now and what you will do are another.

If you do not attend to my words, and depart this life, I shall look down on you from the sky and watch you paying the penalty, lamenting with bitter groans, giving account for all the things you have done.[24] Then you will remember the divine advice I offered to you: none of your horses trained in war, or your hordes of spear-bearers, will follow you there. You will wail and lament for the life you have thrown away on disorder, hurly-burly and battles full of innocent blood, while all around you all you will see is reminders of the evils you have heaped up for yourself. I know the punishment that God inflicts on men. "Yours was good advice, Dandamis", you will say, and you will be right. All round you will stand the souls of those you slaughtered unjustly and to no purpose. How then will you make sufficient amends? It will do you no good to be called "the Great", or to pretend to it: he who set out to conquer the world will be conquered at last.'

31 Alexander was very pleased at what he heard, and was not angry. There was in fact a divine spirit in him, but it had been perverted by an evil demon into slaughter and uproar. He was very struck by Dandamis' paradoxical teaching.

32 'You are a true teacher of the Brahmans', he said, 'and you mould the men who encounter you according to the wisdom of Providence. I heard of you from Calanus and wanted to meet you; but I have found a man superior to all other men thanks to the spirit that is in you. I know that all you say is true. God created you and sent you to this place where you are able to live a blessed life, at peace with all of nature, rich, lacking for nothing, enjoying great tranquillity.

33 'What shall I do, seeing that I live with incessant fears, and drowning in continuous disturbance? How far must I fear those who protect me even more than the enemy? The friends who advise me day by day are worse for me than my enemies: I cannot live without them, but I am never cheerful when I am with them. Those I fear are my protectors. By day I torment the nations, but when night comes on I am tormented by my own

reflections, my fear that someone may come at me with a sword. Ah me: if I punish those who disobey me I am miserable, but if I do not punish them they despise me.

34 'How can I begin to repudiate my actions? If I wanted to live in the wilderness, my troops would not allow me. Even if I could run away, they would not allow me, for such is my allotted fate. What defence shall I make to God who gave me this destiny when I was born?[25]

35 'Please, old man, accept from me the gifts I have brought you, a possession worthy of a god, for the benefit and cheer you have given me with your advice; do not dishonour me by rejecting them. It is a good deed to honour wisdom.'

36 With these words, Alexander made a sign to his slaves. They brought forward gold and silver coins, clothing of all kinds, bread and oil. When Dandamis saw all this he laughed.

37 'Tell the birds who live in the woods to accept the gold and silver, and sing better', he said. 'You will not persuade me to behave worse than the birds. What I cannot eat or drink, I do not accept. I pay no attention to useless goods, nor will I enslave my free soul to no purpose. I have no need to buy things here in the woods. God gives me as a gift the fruit to eat and the water to drink, a forest for a house, air to aid the growth of all things. God does not sell goods for gold, but gives all good things for free. He gives good wits to those who know how to accept them.

38 'I wear the garment in which my mother bore me in her birth pangs. I feed on air and contemplate myself with content. Why compel me to put fetters on my whole body? My natural thirst makes the water of this river sweeter to me than honey. If these loaves are for food, why have you burnt them with fire? I do not eat what has been roasted in fire, nor take away the food of another. Let the fire that has tasted them consume them. But, in order not to dishonour you in honouring wisdom, I will accept the oil.'[26]

39 With these words Dandamis stood up, and moving about the forest he gathered a great pile of wood, lit a fire and, with these words – 'A Brahman possesses all things and is nourished by wisdom' – fanned the flames and poured into it the oil, until it was all consumed. He then sang the following hymn to God.

'Immortal God, I thank you for all things. You alone are the true ruler of all things, and your creation provides abundance of all nourishment. You created this universe, you watch over and wait for the souls you have sent here, so that you may give honour like a god to those who live properly, and hand over to the judgement those who disobey your commandments. All right judgement is in your hands, and eternal life is prepared beside you; in your everlasting goodness you have mercy on everyone.'

40 When Alexander heard and saw all this he was amazed, and cut to the quick by Dandamis' wise and truthful words. He went away carrying all the gifts he had brought with him, except the oil which had been consumed in the fire.

41 'Thus are we all', said Dandamis to him then. 'Calanus was a bad man who for a short time imitated our way of life. But when he did not come closer to God he ran away to the Greeks. Having seen our mysteries under false pretences he polluted them among the nations and surrendered himself to everlasting fire. You, man, whoever you are, who rule over the wicked nation of the Macedonians and were accustomed to revile the Brahmans, and had ordered their extermination – you were persuaded by lying arguments, which it was not fitting for a king, and one who cares for his people, to attend to.

42 'We shall give an account of our lives to God when we depart to meet him; for we belong to him. We despise the vain opinions of the foolish. How can you understand us, living evil lives as you do and ignoring the truly good. We Brahmans remember whence we were born and live according to that nature; we devote our energies to living blameless lives. God has given every mortal his own destiny. We lead our lives in tranquillity, taking care for nothing. Any thought about the

material things of life removes the mind from God; and Providence will ask for an account from each of us, and we shall make recompense for our actions. That is why we rejoice to sit in the wilderness and the forests, until we make our minds entirely pleasing to God; we do not wish the amusements and company of other people to distract our souls from God.

43 'Blessed is he who lacks for nothing. He who wishes to please everybody must be the slave of everybody. We have no need to visit cities, which are meeting places of thieves and seed-beds of wickedness. God has given us large houses, high mountains and shady forests where we can eat the fruits of pure nature and drink water and enjoy quiet rest on leaves, setting aside all need to struggle.

44 'How can you, who are slaves to everything, give orders to those who are free in all things? You are really slaves of your souls, which desire all and everything. If you want to have many cloaks, you need the shepherd; if you want woven garments, you need a fuller and a weaver. Do not say to me, "I do not wear soft garments", for the enslavement is the same whether the matter is great or small. The man who desires a small amount of gold goes on to want more, and the one who desires to rule a small city goes on to want a larger one. You can become greatly luxurious even in a garment dyed with just a little purple, while your slaves are dressed entirely in purple. You regard purple as glorious and wear it very little; but if you have only a little of what is good, you are really poor and dazzled by little things.

45 'Why do you kill animals,[27] seeing that they are children of earth and of greatest use to you? Some of them you shear, some you milk, some are beasts of burden and some you even mount to go to war. And yet you slaughter them; that is the wages the beasts receive from you. Of some of them you wear the fleeces as clothing, of others you digest the flesh within you, and you become walking graves of the creatures. How can a soul burdened with such anomalies be receptive to the mind of God?

Leave off meat for two days and see what will happen: you will not be able to stand the smell, but will shy away from it. How many impurities descend into your soul as a result of eating meat, and enter the kidneys of those who have such desires? That which fattens the body makes the soul waste away. Meat breeds anger and drives away peace. It quenches temperance and awakens unbridledness. It causes vomiting and chronic drunkenness. It puts to flight the divine spirit and makes room for the demon of violence. But the fruits of the trees and the herbs of the river banks breathe out a beautiful scent, and in the wise who dine on them they engender a mind fitting to God and are advantageous to the body. God created them for the nurture of man and his wisdom. Your mind has been destroyed by overeating, and you breathe the breath of wild beasts by filling yourselves with living flesh. You are corrupt buckets of rotting limbs. You are worse than wolves and lions and the most savage beasts; for if wolves could eat fruit they would not look for meat. Bulls, horses, deer and other kinds of animals have an altogether more righteous manner of sustenance than you, feeding on the herbs of the river banks, drinking water, dwelling on the mountains. As a result their natural strength is preserved and their muscles are toughened. Why then do you not imitate these creatures, which are nurtured by the Providence of God?

46 'You use the preparation of sacrifices and the use of fire as an excuse to provide yourselves with food. You look for large quantities of nourishment and indulge in great expense because of your insatiability, and you quickly grow weary of small animals because the pleasure is less substantial. But your labour is in vain and goes to waste. As a result your life is miserable and full of trouble.

47 'We, however, drink only water. In necessity we quench our thirst with the water of springs, which would flow even if we did not drink from them. You, for the sake of the pleasure of your stomachs, devise culinary arts, so that you may burst open your miserable bellies with the variety of cooked food even when you are not hungry. You hunt the skies for love of

pleasure. You strain the sea with nets. You make expeditions to
the mountains in your greed, priding yourselves on the swiftness
of your dogs, and you insult the beasts and call them inhabitants
of a miserable desert, expressing your dissatisfaction with the
dispensation of Providence. Some you pursue, some you hunt
and kill, and when you capture the wildest of them you shut
them in cages and parade them into the city[28] – not in order to
breed from them and produce something useful, but to abuse
and annihilate your fellow creature and work of God, another
man; to bind him in cruel chains and throw him to a beast, or
to stand as spectators while he wrestles with the beasts and dies
a frightful death – he, who shares your nature and is created by
the hand of God. After this, you slay the beast itself and say, "It
was a terrible man-eater." And what is worst of all, you then
eat this beast which has gorged on the flesh and blood of a man,
thus revealing yourselves as more savage than the worst of
beasts, eating yourselves and compounding the heaped up
suffering in your bellies.

48 'You rob the poorest places in order to build your houses
where you may enjoy your cruel digestion in the warm. You
force your intestines to expand, artificially distended with
immoderate indulgence in the eating of flesh and the drinking of
wine. We pray that we may never be thirsty; we really suffer
discomfort when we fill our bodies with too much water. But
you gather in groups to enjoy drinking wine,[29] and do not stop
drinking until you are out of your minds. Then you stretch out
your hands to make libations, and raise your eyes to the sun,
while you have entirely expelled reason from your brains,
deadened as they are with wine. Those who are mad are more
fortunate than you then, since they can become drunk without
buying wine. You worry about the price of wine because you
want to buy it and drive out your wits with drunkenness and
induce madness; then you set upon each other and inflict harm
on your companions. And you do all this in a state of insensibil-
ity. When the effect of the wine wears off you realise what you

have done to each other from the pain. Yet even this does not keep you away from drinking.

49 'Then, again, you eat so much that you are unable to digest it. On your way home, late, you vomit up your excess through your mouth, thus turning nature topsy-turvy. You drink so immoderately that you are filled up like buckets, and because the wine stinks at last you vomit it up again. In your foolishness you turn your bodies upside down, walking on your heads instead of your feet, like animals. You fill yourselves by force and void yourselves offensively. When you fall sick you massage your body and are vexed at the care with which you have to treat your stomach. When you are always satiated you are deprived of every pleasure. The conclusion of immoderate appetite is not health but the torture of the body. You are punished with diseases because of your immoderation. What use is the luxury of the body towards the happiness of the soul? If you want to demonstrate that you have much, make a present of the excess to those who are in need; but as we hear you are so poor that you cannot even give bread to those who ask you for it. You struggle to accumulate countless possessions, because you are slaves of your bodies and your insatiable innards.

50 'For these reasons there are many doctors among you, who purge your insatiable appetites, or strangle your greed with fasting and bridle disease with other arts, or tame with thirst those who formerly poured wine into their bodies as if into a leaky bucket, and do not allow them even a drop of water. Under this treatment, those who suffered with headaches are dried out. Formerly they drank wine, which is against nature, but now water, which is in accordance with nature. Formerly they were shackled to insatiable appetite, but now they are bound to the continence of necessity like broken limbs to a splint.

51 'Brahmans do not require wine. We have the water we want, and enjoy it. We assuage our thirst rationally. We do not inflict madness on ourselves. We would rather die than be overcome

by drunkenness. It is better to be thrown to a wild beast than to fall away from God through inebriation. The drunken man lives like a dead man, with the loss of his wits and alienated from God.

52 'What of those who are great among you? Deceived by wealth, they goggle at a lie and because they think that they have only what is here they commit injustice, they kill the weak and deprive them even of the little they own. And at the end of all this waits Death.

53 'What shall we say about the Epicureans,[30] men drenched in perfume who go about dressed in soft clothes like women and polluting the air with artificial scents? What shall we say about the Stoics[31] and their love of money? Yet all these are great and admired among you.

54 'We hear that you castrate males and make them into females. So you have a human being who can neither engender like a man nor give birth like a woman, and lives only for his own unbridledness. Who would not pity you when they see such destruction among you?

55 'Through our pity we may help you not to succumb to your own current opinions. So, though we hate arrogance, we love all human nature, and we set ourselves before you as teachers of the truth and guides along the way of justice for all those who are willing to be benefited by us in this life, as in a great house; our souls are as naked as our bodies, and so the wealth of our entire souls is apparent to every man.

56 'We hear that Macedonia, formerly a victim, now attacks everyone. They are all slaves of their souls' urgings. But the Brahmans have no part in any of this, since we are at war with no one and desire nothing.

57 'If you wish to think like us, come and join us and live naked in the wilderness; that is the only way we will accept you. Then you will be just a man and no one will make war on you any more; and no one will be able to take anything away from you.

When the forest is your nourisher you will have all the wealth you need. That is the gift the Brahmans will give you, since you wrote to me to ask for help. We bear no malice against those who truly wish to be pious, but we imitate God who has mercy on every human creature.'

5
The Correspondence of
Alexander and Dindimus

News has reached me from many sources that your way of life and customs are very different from those of other men. I have also heard that you seek no assistance either by land or by sea. If this is true, you are very remarkable men. Because what I have recently heard about you is very hard to believe, I am writing to you, Dindimus, to question you as to whether what I have heard is true and whether it is a product of your wisdom. Please inform me so that I can know for sure; then I too, if possible, shall follow your way of life. Ever since I was a child I have enjoyed learning. Our own wise men teach us to live well, so that our lives shall not meet with reproach. But I have heard that you adhere to a doctrine which excels that taught by our sages in its wisdom. So my message is a request to send me your teaching without delay, as this can be no loss to you and may perhaps be of great use to us. It is a good and useful practice that men should share with one another, and no man suffers any loss in his goodness when he does good to another, however he does it. It is just as if one man were carrying a lit torch and other men were to come and light other torches from the first: it would not lose its own light. So it is with goodness. Therefore, as I said, send me without delay that which I request of you.

[DINDIMUS' FIRST REPLY]

I have learnt from you, Alexander, what it is you wish to discover, namely perfect wisdom, even though you are – as we know – already very wise. Nonetheless, I heartily applaud your desire to learn what is best in every kingdom. An emperor who does not know wisdom cannot rule others but becomes their servant. Still, it seems to me hard, if not impossible, for you to adhere to our way of life and customs, because your education is so different from ours. I would have preferred to maintain silence and to ask your pardon in this matter concerning which you have sent me your request, since it will be of no advantage for me to describe our life and customs: you will have no time to read my letter, busy as you are with waging wars. But, so that you may not be able to say I refused you through malice, I will write to you as much as I can about this matter you ask about. You were inclined to disbelieve the messenger who brought you information about us; perhaps you will be more able to learn the truth, without doubts, from me personally. From this letter you will learn who we are who lead this blessed life.

We are Brahmans. We lead a simple, pure life, commit no crimes, and have no desire for more than is proportionate to our nature. We endure and put up with all things. We give the name of necessary to what is not superfluous. We have an abundance of the food that nature provides. We seek to consume no other food than that which mother earth produces without labour. We fill our tables with such food as cannot harm us, and as a result we are without sickness and remain healthy as long as we live. We make no medicines, we seek no support for our bodily health. We have no love of riches, and there is no envy amongst us. None among us is stronger than another, and our poverty is for us riches because we have everything in common. We have no courts, because we commit no crimes which would compel us to go to law. Any law would be contrary to our nature, because we ask no one's pity, for the reason that we do not even give any cause why we should seek another's pity. We do not forgive anyone else's sins in order that God should for that reason forgive us our sins, nor do we give riches in compensation for our sins. We do no work which is associated with the desire for gain. We do not surrender our bodies to lust; we commit no adultery, nor engage in any other vice of which we should be ashamed. It is forbidden among us to plough the fields with a plough or to yoke oxen to a cart. We do not fill our bellies with quantities of food nor drop nets into the sea to catch fish. We do not go hunting after birds or four-footed beasts, nor do we bring home their hides. Cupidity is insatiable and the cause of men sinking into poverty, because they cannot make an end of getting: for the more a greedy man has, the more he wants to have.

We do not have baths nor wash our bodies in hot water. Why should we wash our bodies when there is nothing impure on them? The sun gives us heat and we are washed with the dew. When we are thirsty, we drink the water of the river. Our beds are the earth; when we sleep, we sleep without cares. We do not go in for meditation. We have no servants: we have no dominion over men, who are just like we are. Besides, it is cruel to press a man into slavery whom nature has decreed to be our brother, and who has been created by the same heavenly father as we are.

We do not fashion stones into blocks to build ourselves houses, nor do we make vessels or tiles of clay. We set no foundations for palaces, because we live in ditches or in the caves of the mountains, where no sound of the wind is heard and we need fear no rain. Our houses are such that, while we are alive, we live in them, and when we die, they become our tombs.

We dye no clothing with varied colours; in fact we do not cover our bodies, for we are not ashamed of them. Our women do not adorn themselves to please men; they regard such ornaments as a burden, because they know that beauty is not in ornaments but in the nature with which they were born. Who, after all, can change the work of nature? If anyone does try to change it, that is to be reprehended, either because it is not properly done or because it will not last.

We have no lawsuits, never resort to weapons; our pacifism is a matter of habit, not of virtue. We do not complain of the fates, because we do everything in proper manner. We do not succumb to death until the due age is on us, because we have all learnt to die equally. We do not adorn our sepulchres, nor place the ashes of our sons in jewel-encrusted urns. What could be of less value than bones, which the earth must receive again? You burn them rather than scattering them so that the earth which generated them may receive them again, and you build splendid sepulchres for wretched men. Let men learn what rewards you bestow on your lovers.

You say that Asia and Africa come to an end after a little distance. You show man how to sail on the terrible Ocean. You eat constantly and always look hungry. You commit adultery with your mothers. You sow discord between kings. Among you, the humble are made proud. You commit many crimes because of your gods, who did just the same: it is a proof of the power of your god Jupiter, and of Proserpine, whom you worship, that he committed adultery with many women, and that she caused many men to descend into hell. You do not allow your free men to receive honours, but you treat your servants like noblemen. Your judges are not just. You make your judges change the law and you practise and indulge all the vices that you have. But the wisdom of the Brahmans is superior to you in every respect, because, in our opinion, the same mother bore both you and the precious stones.

We Brahmans do not suffer sudden death, because we do not corrupt the air with dirty deeds, which commonly cause pestilence. We do not go in for amusements; if we wish to learn anything of an amusing nature, we read about what your ancestors did and what you yourselves do; and while we are compelled to laugh at them, we bewail them also. But we do see other things which both amaze us and give us pleasure, as follows: we see the sky resplendent with stars, the sun glowing in his aerial chariot and his rays illumining the whole world. We see the sea maintain its constant dark hue; and when it is roused by tempests, it does not overwhelm the neighbouring land but embraces it like a sister; and every day we can see the various kinds of fish, and the dolphins leaping and sporting in its waves. We delight in seeing the fields in flower, and the sweet scents which rise from them to our nostrils, so that our eyes are satiated with the sight as well as our bodies; and we enjoy all places where there are groves and springs, and love to hear the birds sing. We are always full of wonder at these things.

Such are the customs which come naturally to us, though you will find them hard to adhere to; but if you do not follow them, so much the worse for you.

We do not put out to sea to engage in commerce, nor do we send goods to distant lands where those who go there will undergo many dangers and learn of other wonders. We do not study the art of speaking well, but do so naturally; all our speech is imbued with that simplicity which forbids us to lie. We do not attend the schools of philosophers, in whose teachings there is disagreement and nothing has a sure and certain definition; in fact it is all lies. Instead we attend those schools in which we can learn to live well, which will demonstrate what is written down here; which will not teach us to harm others, but will teach us to live according to true justice, and where we shall learn nothing that will cause us any kind of sadness.

We do not kill cattle in honour of the gods nor build temples in which to place a gold or silver statue of some god or other. You, however, have the custom of honouring the gods with all your possessions, to force them to listen to you. You do not understand that God will not listen to any man for the price of gifts, or of the blood of calves, or of boars, or of sheep. God loves nothing except good works, so he will listen to a man who prays with words, for in words at least man resembles God, since God is the Word. And that Word created the earth, and through that Word all have life. We worship this Word and adore it and love it, for it is God the Spirit and Mind. Therefore it loves nothing but a pure mind. For this reason we regard you as utterly deluded since you have no idea what your heavenly nature is and how it shares in the nature of God; instead you pollute yourselves and your nature with adultery and fornication and the service of idols. The result of your behaviour, in which you engage constantly, is that you are impure as long as you live and, after your death, you are subject to further torments.

You hope to propitiate your god with the flesh and blood which you offer to him. But you do not serve the one god who reigns in heaven, but many gods. You worship as many gods as there are organs in the human body. You call Juno the goddess of the heart, that is, she is your goddess of anger. Mars, because he was the god of battles, is regarded by you as the god of the chest. Mercury, because he talked a lot, is regarded by you as the god of the tongue. Hercules, moreover, because of his twelve labours, is regarded by you as the god of the arms. Bacchus, because he was the god of drunkenness, is regarded by you as the god of the throat, and as standing guard over the throat as he does over a cellar of wine. Ceres, because she was the goddess of grain, is regarded by you as the goddess of the stomach. Venus, who was the goddess of fornication, is regarded by you as the goddess of the genital organs. You call Jupiter the god of the nose because you say that he holds the breath of the air. You call Apollo the god of the hands because he first invented medicine and music. In fact, you divide the whole of the human body up among the gods, and do not grasp that your bodies were created by one god, who is in heaven.

Each of these gods whom you worship has his own special area, whether it be birds or grain or some other object; so how can you say that they have power in your own bodies? They have no power except over the animals which are offered to them.

Certainly you deserve the promised torments you will endure after death on account of your errors. In truth, the gods you pray to are not helpers but butchers, who divide up your limbs according to various torments. Your bodies will in fact have to suffer as many torments as you claim there are gods holding sway over those bodies.

One god makes you fornicate, another makes you eat, another drink, another go to law. They all give you orders and you serve them all, worship them all. Your wretched body ought to be worn out with the amount of service you pay to all these gods. It is proper that you should serve gods of this kind, in view of the great evils you do and your refusal to cease from evils: that is why you serve such gods. You have no reason to serve gods who order you to do such evil things. If those gods of yours listen to you when you call on them, they do damage to your conscience; but if they do not listen to you, they will oppose your own desire, since you never ask them for anything but evil. Therefore, whether they listen to you or not, they always do you harm. These are your gods known as the Furies, who avenge the sins of men through their rage after death. These are those torments of which your learned men have taught you, which torture you even in life as though you were already dead. If you will consider well, you will see that no one can suffer worse in hell than you suffer now, and that you yourselves are the phantoms whose existence you describe in the underworld. There are punishments in hell, and you will suffer punishment as long as you go hunting after adultery and fornication. They say that Tantalus is in hell, always thirsty and never satisfied; but your desire is of such a kind that you likewise can never be satisfied. They say that Cerberus, the three-headed dog, is in hell; but if you think about it, you will see that your belly is a Cerberus because of its excessive eating and drinking. Then, again, they say there is in hell the serpent Hydra: you could be called Hydras on account of the numerous vices with which you indulge your bellies. And all the other things too which are supposed to be in hell are, if you look at it rightly, aspects of yourself in your wickedness. Alas, for you, wretched creatures, who adhere to a faith that ensures you such torments after death!

ALEXANDER'S REPLY TO DINDIMUS

If all these things are as you say, dear Dindimus, then the Brahmans must be the only good men, and so far removed from ordinary bad men who refrain from bad actions, as not even to have a disposition to do those things which are characteristic of human nature. You say that everything we do is sinful, that all our arts are sins; you wish to destroy all the customs which human nature up until now has followed. You must either think that you are gods yourselves or have some grudge against our gods. Therefore it is my opinion that your life and customs are closer to stupidity than to wisdom.

DINDIMUS REPLIED

We are not dwellers in this world here as if we expected to be here for ever; rather we are sojourners, here for a temporary visit. We are on our way to the house of our fathers. We are not weighed down by our sins, and we do not stay in the tabernacles of sinfulness. We do nothing secretly but, because of our good conscience, go about in public. We do not regard ourselves as gods, nor do we have a grudge against God; but we do not do things which are against God. God, who created everything in the world, acted so that the world could not stand without a great variety of things, and gave man judgement in order to distinguish between the things that are in the world. Therefore, whoever abjures the worse and follows the better is not a god but a friend of God. We ourselves, who live in a holy and continent manner, would have no reason to regard ourselves as gods or to bear a grudge against God. That suspicion which you entertain of us is truer of yourselves. When you are so inflated with excessive prosperity, you forget that you are only born of man.

Then again, you say that God does not care for human affairs. You build yourselves temples, you set up altars and are delighted when the cattle are slaughtered there and your name is attached to the sacrifice. This one is killed for your father, that one for your grandfather or the rest of your relations. Therefore I am right in saying that you are all mad, since you do not know what it is you do. And so you want to attach to us, who see clearly, the darkness of your own blindness, and will not allow us to lament your misery. A man can help a lost soul in as much as he laments for him. Anyone who does not acknowledge that he is mortal receives honours of the same kind as Salmoneus and Enceladus, who are confined in hell, according to the stories of the philosophers.

ALEXANDER'S REPLY

So, dear Dindimus, you say you are blessed because you happen to have your dwelling in that part of the world where no stranger can come to you, nor can you leave it. You remain as if imprisoned in that region and, since you cannot get rid of your land, you praise it, and say that you endure the sufferings you do endure simply out of continence. According to your doctrine, even those who are shut up in prison ought to be called blessed, because they endure a life of punishment in prison until old age: for that is no different from what you are saying. Even the goods which you say you have are like the tortures of those in prison, and you endure of your own free will that which our law prescribes for condemned criminals. In other words, anyone who among you is called a sage would among us be called a criminal; so it would certainly be appropriate for us to lament your miseries and sigh for your sufferings. What worse affliction can there be for a man than to be forbidden to live at liberty? God did not wish us to undergo punishment for ever, but decreed that you should undergo these trials while you are alive. So, although you call yourselves philosophers, you earn no need of praise for it.

Rather, I insist that your life is not blessedness but punishment. If you like, I will enumerate various points concerning your life. You say that the Brahmans do not have the custom of sowing seeds, nor planting vines or trees, nor building fine buildings. The reason for this is quite obviously that you have no iron with which you could do the things I have mentioned. Then, again, you cannot sail ships; therefore you have to eat grass and live the rough life of cattle. But do not even wolves do this? When they cannot hunt meat for food, they satisfy themselves on a meagre diet of herbs. If you were able to come to our country, I should have no need of your wisdom concerning penury, since that penury would remain in your country; while if we were to travel to your poverty-stricken land, we should have made ourselves paupers. There is nothing to admire in a man's living in poverty and want, but rather in living temperately in the midst of riches. The only glory to be found in blindness and poverty is that blindness does not see what it lacks and poverty has no way of getting it.

You say that your women wear no ornaments, and that there is no fornication or adultery among you. It would be cause for amazement if you were to practise this restraint voluntarily; but in fact you do it because you find no pleasure in the appearance of your women, unadorned as they are; you remain chaste because of the absence of any stimulus to be otherwise. You say that you have no interest in study and that you require no pity nor pity others. All these are things you have in common with the beasts, which, because they are unable to recognise what is good, take no pleasure in anything good. But we rational men, who have free will, have been provided by nature with many comforts to improve our lives. It would be impossible for this great world not to have something to temper and moderate it, for there to be no happiness to offset grief. If human inclinations are diverse, and alter under different skies, so also the mind of man has many facets, and when the day is darkened then men become sad. Likewise, the sensibilities of men change with the seasons. In infancy he rejoices in simple things, while the youth is impetuous and the old man is sluggish and indecisive. Who looks for wisdom in a little boy, or constancy in a young man, or swift-footedness in an old man? There are many pleasant things of which we can make use, whether they appeal to our sight, or our hearing, or to smell, taste or touch. Sometimes we enjoy dancing, sometimes singing; at other times we like to enjoy pleasant odours or sweet tastes or a gentle touch. Given that we have all the good fruits of the earth, and the abundance of the fish of the sea, and the delicacies of the birds that fly, your wish that we should abstain from all things will lead to your being judged either over-proud, for despising all these gifts, or envious, because you think I have been endowed with better gifts than you.

6

Alexander the Great's Journey
to Paradise

So Alexander, loaded up with all kinds of fine booty, stole away from Indian territory, accompanied by his troops. He had with him plenty of supplies, and halted the army at the next suitable quarters, on a promontory between the river and the nearby sea. He wanted to allow the army some rest to recover their strength after the trials and dangers they had undergone. Wherever he travelled, he was received with warmth and honour. Everyone offered him their service, impressed alike by his generosity and kindness and because he restrained his troops from pillaging their possessions. They regarded it as a sign of superiority in a prince that his companions should turn out to be peaceful and well-disposed, when they had expected them to come as enemies and thieves.

In due course Alexander came to a very wide river, on the bank of which he came upon a ship of considerable size, complete with sails and oars, as well as a multitude of weapons and tackle of all kinds, and in good sailing order. He inquired the name of the river and was told that it was the Ganges, also known as Physon, whose source is in the paradise of earthly bliss.[1] He also saw houses roofed with immense leaves, which float down the river and are brought to shore by the inhabitants with long poles; they dry them in the sun and pound them to a powder, thus producing a spice of wonderful savour.

When Alexander had learnt all this, and had also investigated the origins and location of the place, he sighed and said, 'I have achieved nothing so far in this world, and I shall regard all my ambitious quest as vain if I do not manage to win a share of this bliss.'

Immediately, having ensured that his troops were safely

positioned, he selected 500 foot soldiers in peak condition –
energetic, undeterred by any danger and willing to endure
unremitting toil – loaded the ship with sufficient supplies for the
whole summer, and set sail, entrusting his fate to the prosperous
winds. Their intention was, if it should be permitted, to reach
the source of the river. They sailed for a month, proceeding with
considerable difficulty against the strong current. But at this
time the strength of the men began to fail, despite their constant
mutual exhortations and their efforts to outdo each other at the
work. Pretty soon it was clear that it would be impossible to go
further: they were worn out with the beating of the waves that
washed over them and nearly deaf from the incredible roar of
the breakers, so that none of them could hear the voice of his
companion unless he yelled loudly. Then at length, on the thirty-
fourth day, they saw in the distance what appeared to be a
walled city of remarkable height and extent. They approached it
with great difficulty. Near the shore, the river ran somewhat less
fiercely and the noise of the waves was a little less; but the
narrowness of the shore and the muddy ground prevented them
from advancing on foot to the wall. They therefore continued to
sail for almost three days, with great difficulty, along the side of
the city where it stretched from its northern extremity towards
the south, looking for a way in.

The wall was very smooth, with no towers or ramparts in its
circuit. The entire surface was covered with ancient moss, so
that the stones and their joins were completely invisible. On the
third day they caught sight of a tiny window shuttered on the
inside, a sight which instantly relieved the spirits and strength of
the tired travellers with hope.

Alexander immediately had some of his men embark in a boat
to see if anyone might answer when they knocked, and gave
them a message for the inhabitants. As soon as they reached the
wall they knocked loudly and shouted to those inside to open
up. After a time they heard someone slide the bolt, and a gentle
voice inquired of them who they were and where they had come
from, and asked them to explain their unusual and unheard-of
demand.

'We are messengers of no ordinary king', they replied, 'but of the king of kings, Alexander the unconquered, to whom all the world pays homage, before whom every power trembles. This is the message his majesty sends you, after consultation with his chief nobles: "What kind of people live in this place, and what laws do they follow? How numerous are they? What are their defences? Who is their king and by what hope does he live? What faith does he profess? What forces can he rely on?" Our lord also orders you: "If you wish to continue to enjoy your hope of life, your bodily safety, and quiet times, do not puff yourselves up with insolence but pay me tribute according to the custom of all other peoples of the world."'

The listener was not troubled by their words but replied with a cheerful expression and a gentle voice, 'Do not wear yourselves out with multiplying threats and piling up demands; wait patiently and I shall be with you shortly.'

So saying, he closed the window. After about two hours, he opened it again and showed himself to the waiting sailors. He held out a jewel of unusual colour and remarkable brilliance, which in size and shape much resembled a human eye. He handed it to the men and said, 'The inhabitants of this place send this message to your king: "Call it whatever you like, a gift or a tribute owed, but accept a memento in the gift of this remarkable stone, which we send to you as a kind of charitable alms. It has the power to take away all your longings. When you have learnt its nature and its virtue, you will cease from all ambition. You will know also that it is not expedient for you and your companions to remain longer here, since if the river should be stirred by even a moderate storm, your ship will without doubt be wrecked and all your lives will be lost. Therefore, return to your companions, and try not to be ungrateful to the god of gods for the benefits conferred on you."' He ceased speaking, closed up the aperture and withdrew.

The men quickly returned to the ship, bringing Alexander the jewel and the message. He, being a wise man, reflected on the event and weighed the man's words, and returned with all speed to familiar shores and his own encampment. His men were delighted at his return, which they had been anxiously anticipating. Indeed for some time they had been doubtful whether he would ever return alive. When they heard what had occurred they poured out their congratulations and their gratitude at his safe return. They heard all about the manifold dangers of the fast-flowing river, the men's deafness and the frequent inundations of the waters, the speed and violence of the current and the intolerable roar of the waves; and they rejoiced that their leader, though he had despaired of his strength many times, had overcome all these perils successfully.

Thence they advanced to the wealthy city of Susa,[2] where they were received with full royal honours and the oldest men were particularly richly honoured. Many of the tallest men honoured the imperial nobility with splendid gifts and they withdrew no less laden with royal rewards.

On the next day Alexander summoned secretly several of the wisest men of the Jews and gentiles, from whom he knew he could expect a reliable answer. He told them the tale of his adventure and the mysterious meeting at the window, and then brought out the jewel and asked them to explain its nature and virtue. They, however, could offer no certain opinion on the mystery; all they could do was praise the man's good fortune, rejoice in the outcome and extol his power. They asked for time to study the puzzle. Alexander was displeased at this but concealed his frustration. He showed no scorn for the ignorance and simplicity of the men, but presented them with royal gifts.

There was in that place a very aged Jew by the name of Papas,[3] who was so frail as a result of his length of years that he could only go from place to place in a litter carried by two men. When he heard from his friends about the king's adventure, and that he was troubled with anxiety about the mystery of the stone, he begged to be brought into the king's presence. When Alexander saw him, he displayed his customary respect to the man's grey hairs, and seated the old gentleman comfortably beside him. He congratulated him on his long life and on his handsome and distinguished appearance, and, as was his pleasant custom with the elderly, began to discuss the events of olden times. The old man's satisfactory answers indicated to Alexander that he was seated next to a veritable ocean of wisdom, and so he began to relate the story of his expedition, its many hardships and its eventual successful outcome.

But the Jew, when he heard of the successful voyage and its fortunate outcome, so far beyond what one might have expected, raised up his hands and cried out before everyone present, 'Your majesty, do not neglect to consider at all times how much you are indebted to the God of Heaven! To no mortal has he allowed such a privilege. The success of the venture is not due to fate, but to the generosity of God. I remember when I was a boy that some young men of great strength and intelligence undertook this voyage, but they were in no way able to approach the walls of that city, and even so they almost all came back incapacitated. Some of them were exhausted by the excessive toil and were washed overboard by the waves; others went blind, or deaf, or were permanently disabled by a trembling of the limbs. After that, various others made the attempt at various times, but their labour was in vain, for they were all disabled in various ways and scarcely escaped with their lives. It is a long time since that people gave up this vain attempt. By what dispensation of the fates, then, have you and your companions overcome the ferocity of the waves, reached that city which until now was innocent of all visitors, and received a response allowed to no other mortal? In truth, the explanation must lie in the permission or dispensation of God, or it is thanks to a great wonder.'

These remarks brought Alexander out of his former disconsolate puzzlement. He replied cheerfully, 'What the Scripture says is true, that there is wisdom in the old. Your statement agrees with the spiritual mystery which was conveyed to me in a prophetic utterance by the inhabitants of that city. I have wasted a great deal of time with the wise men of this place in trying to elucidate that wonder whose existence you have divined.' Then he opened his hand to display the jewel. 'Here', he said, 'is the very object of your conjecture.'

The Jew took the jewel and looked at it for a long time. 'This is indeed a wonder', he said, 'and a memento which is not unworthy of the royal dignity.'

'Since your opinion is just that of him who gave it to me', said Alexander, 'do not torture me with suspense. If you know anything about it, explain it to me, and release me from my ignorance of its riddle.'

'Although much reliability attaches to prophetic utterances', replied the Jew, 'the sense of sight is often more susceptible of persuasion concerning some new thing than that of hearing. This stone is of moderate size, but of immense weight; in fact nothing could equal its mass. Bring me a pair of scales and a pound of gold.'

This was done immediately, and the old man placed the stone in one pan and a gold coin in the other: the stone outweighed it and the pan with the coin shot up. He added the rest of the coins one by one, until the whole pound was in the pan, and then as much gold as the pan would hold, without being able to budge the stone in the slightest from its lower position. Then they sent for the largest pair of scales in the place, attached it to a beam and loaded it with many hundreds of gold coins; but the stone, just as it had done with the first coin, lifted the whole lot swiftly into the air, as if it had been not a load of gold but a tiny feather in the pan.

When Alexander saw this, which was so far beyond what he would have believed possible, he said in astonishment, 'I am really amazed that this little jewel, which seems when held in the hand to weigh almost nothing, appears so heavy as soon as it is placed on the scales. Now, however, that seeing this sight has persuaded me of what I should never have believed had it been told me, please explain in words this novel mystery.'

'Wait patiently, your majesty', replied the Jew, 'until the demonstration is completed in proper form, and then I will explain the puzzle to your satisfaction.'

He took again the smaller pair of scales, in which they had piled so much weight, and on the one side he placed the stone, this time covering it with a light film of dust, while on the other side he placed one gold coin. Immediately the coin sank and pulled the stone upwards with no trouble at all. The Jew took out the coin and replaced it with a feather; but still it exceeded the stone in weight.

Alexander was practically fainting with amazement. 'Never', he said, 'anywhere in the world have I heard of such a thing, nor seen such a thing, nor even dreamt of it.'

'The demonstration is now complete', stated the Jew, 'and now follows the verbal explanation of the mystery concealed herein.'

'Please,' said Alexander, 'since I am very disturbed by the riddle attaching to the city I saw, and its inhabitants, explain it to me in every detail.'

Having thus whetted their curiosity, the Jew turned to face the whole crowd and broke his silence as follows: 'What you have seen, your majesty, is not a city and should not be called one. It is a solid wall, impenetrable to all mortal flesh, which the Creator of all things placed there to bar all further progress, for the benefit of the spirits of the just now freed from the flesh and awaiting the resurrection of the body. There they enjoy a dim repose, which God has decreed for them – but not for ever, because after the Judgement they will receive their flesh again and reign with the Creator for eternity. These spirits, who are enthusiastic for human salvation, sent you this stone as a memento of your blessed fortune, both to protect you and to constrain the inordinate and inappropriate urgings of your ambition. If you think about it, what advantage is there in insatiable longing, which consumes the mind with constant anxiety and tortures it with suspicion and distrust? It leads a rational man to use up all his quietness, makes him the ignoble slave of his own slave, and compels him to join night to day in the contemplation of his worries.

'However, if you will be content to stay in your own home and enjoy the sufficiency of your inheritance, your royal state will never come to an end: you will be at peace and divested of all care, while the wealth and riches of your kingdom will be your servants and the abundance of every treasury will pour itself into your coffers. At the moment, however, you are content neither with your own wealth nor with that of others; in the midst of your treasure-houses you are oppressed with want, nothing is enough for you, and, at great peril to your life and to that of those around you, you weigh yourself down with the ill-gotten burden of others' riches.

'This advice forms the essence of the mystery which is contained in this wondrous stone. As far as its shape and colour are concerned, it is indeed a human eye, which, for as long as it has access to the light of life, is constantly agitated with the heat of desire; it grazes on the multiplicity of novelties and, even as gold ministers to its ever-renewing hunger, it never reaches any kind of satiety.[4] The more it manages to increase its holdings, so much the more diligently does it devote itself to piling up more. That is the meaning of the magical effect of the stone's weight. But as soon as its vital motion is removed, and it is commended to the keeping of the earth from which it was born, it is beyond the use of any useful thing, it enjoys nothing, it desires nothing, it is unmoved by any external stimulus, because it is without feeling. Thus even a light feather, be it never so small, so long as it is useful for something, is able to outweigh the stone once it is covered with dust.

'This stone is you, your majesty, you — the master of all wisdom, the conqueror of kings, the possessor of kingdoms, the lord of the world; the stone is your counsellor, your castigator; its little substance shall keep you from the yearnings of shoddy ambition. This is what I have to say, saving your grace, my lord and king, and if it seems that I have exceeded the bounds of the honour due to a king in my cautionary speech, it is because I yielded in my unwisdom to your imperial command.'

Alexander delayed not a moment but rushed to embrace the old man. He sent him home laden with royal gifts, praying for his prosperity and safety. At once he put an end to his own desires and ambitions and made room for the exercise of generosity and noble behaviour. He became the most liberal-handed of kings, as befitted his royal glory, both towards his intimates and to everyone else.

He departed from there and travelled through the extent of the lands which were under his rule. Here and there he was detained by the necessity of dispensing justice, but after a circuit of another half a year he reached Babylon. Here, as if he had returned home after his many adventures and trials, he gave himself up to a quiet and peaceful life, allowing the companions of his journey to go into retirement, and endowing each of them according to the quality of his service with quantities of gold and silver.

All malicious envy had been dispelled. He flourished in magnificence and rejoiced in his royal glory. But one day he was killed by a poisoned cup, administered by one of his domestic servants, whom he least suspected – just as he had been told in India by the oracular trees of the Sun and Moon. As the poison penetrated into his veins and he felt death coming on, he summoned the young men who had been his pages and school companions, and divided the administration of his kingdom among them. He established the limits of his empire. He confirmed the duties of the army in the regular increase of peace and concord. He impressed on all the need to pursue truth, nobility and generosity and instructed them in the imitation of his own model of virtue. Then, saying farewell to each one in turn, he brought to an end his last day. Alleluia.

The end of the life of King Alexander the Great.

APPENDIX I: BERLIN PAPYRUS 13044

'. . . [whoever] I command to judge, he shall be your moderator; if I decide that he has judged well, he alone shall be let off alive.'

One of the gymnosophists asked if they should set a penalty as well. This one having volunteered to go first, Alexander asked him whether he considered that the living were more numerous than the dead, or the reverse. He replied that the living were.

'Is it not proper', he asked, 'that those who exist should be more numerous than those who do not?'

Then he asked the next whether the earth [or the sea is greater]. The reply was that [the earth is greater] because the sea itself is upon the earth.

He asked the third which he took to be the most cunning of all living creatures.

'That which no man has yet discovered.'

He asked the fourth why he had incited Sabeilos to fight against him; the reply came: 'In order that he should succeed in either living nobly or dying nobly.'

He ordered the fifth to state which came first, day or night. He replied that the day came first, by a single night.

While Alexander was trying to work this out, the Indian noticed and remarked that the answers to riddling questions were likely to be just as riddling.

He asked the sixth what a man should do to make himself most loved by men. He replied: 'By being all-powerful yet frightening nobody.'

He asked the seventh what a man should do in order to become a god. He replied: 'By doing what it is impossible for a man to do.'

He asked the eighth which is stronger, death or life. He answered life, because it makes something that exists out of what does not exist, whereas death makes something that does not exist out of what does.

He ordered the last to say how long it is good for a man to live. He replied: 'As long as [he does not regard death as better than life.]'

There was now only one left, [Alexander] asked him to judge the answers, and to state which had given the worst answer: 'I do not want you to think that I shall be neglectful in giving you your reward.'

But the Indian did not want anyone to perish as a result of his answer, so he replied that each had answered worse than the other.

'Well then', said Alexander, 'you shall all die, and you first because it was your judgement.'

'But Alexander', replied the other, 'it is not a kingly act to lie. You said, whoever I shall [appoint judge, if I consider he has judged well, he shall live. . . .] Your statement will . . . us. It is not for us to kill unjustly, but for you to preserve.'

When Alexander heard that, he judged that the men were indeed wise; he ordered them all to be given a cloak and sent them away unharmed.

APPENDIX II: EARLY ENGLISH VERSIONS OF THE LEGENDS

(i) From THE THORNTON 'LIFE OF ALEXANDER'
(ed. J. S. Westlake, EETS 143 (1913); modernised by RS)

Alexander's army in the perilous lands

As they went along this river, about the eighth hour of the day, they came to a castle that stood on a little island in the aforesaid river. This castle was made of the aforesaid reeds. The breadth of this river was four furlongs. In that castle they saw a few men. Then Alexander bade his men ask those who were in the castle, in the language of India, where they might find any sweet water to drink. But as soon as they spoke to them, the people withdrew and hid. Alexander had his men shoot arrows into the castle; but those inside only hid themselves even better.

When Alexander saw that they did not want to speak to him at all, he had some of his knights strip off and swim across the water to the castle. So 37 bold and hardy knights of Macedon stripped, took each a sword in his hand, entered the water and swam until they were most of the way across. Suddenly there rose out of the water a great multitude of beasts, that were called ypotaynes [hippopotamuses], larger in size than an elephant, and devoured every one of the knights. Then Alexander was extremely grieved, and he had the guides taken and thrown into the water. And at once the hippopotamuses devoured them.

Alexander thought it was not sensible to struggle further with these monsters. He had the trumpet sounded and removed his host from that place; and so they went all day, dreadfully faint from thirst. They also had great trouble and disturbance from the wild beasts that came upon them, including lions, bears, unicorns, tigers and leopards, with which they fought hard.

So they went on in this way, full of anger and distress. About the eleventh hour they saw a little boat in the river, made of reeds, with men rowing in it. Alexander asked them in the language of India where they might find any fresh water. They told him where, and showed them a place a little way off where they said they would find a great lake of good fresh water. Then Alexander and his host went along that river until they came to the aforesaid lake and camped around it. Alexander commanded his men to fell a wood that grew close by; it was about three miles long and the same in breadth. It consisted entirely of the reeds that I spoke of before, and the lake was a mile in length. Then Alexander commanded his army to make many fires, and sounded the trumpet for the meal.

As soon as the moon began to shine there came a great multitude of scorpions towards the lake to drink. Then there came other kinds of adders, and dragons, wondrously large, of divers colours. All the country resounded with the noise and the hissing that they made. The dragons came down from the mountains to drink of the lake. They had crests on their heads, their breasts were bright like gold, and their mouths were open. Their breath slew any living thing that it touched, and out of their eyes came flames of fire. When Alexander and his host saw them they were very afraid: they thought they would have to fight them all off. But Alexander comforted them, saying, 'My worshipful knights, do not be afraid of them, but each of you do as you see me do.' And then he took a net and set it between him and them, and took his shield and spear, and fought with them manfully. When his knights saw that, they were greatly comforted; they took their weapons and did as they saw Alexander do; and they killed a great many of them, either with their weapons or in the fires. And the dragons slew 20 of Alexander's knights and 30 of his foot soldiers.

After the dragons there came out of the aforesaid wood of reeds crabs of wondrous size: their beaks were harder than crocodiles'. When the knights smote them on their beaks with their spears, they could not pierce them or harm them in any way. Nevertheless, they slew many of them in their fires, and the remnant of them escaped into the lake.

About the sixth hour of the night there came upon them white lions larger than bulls, and they shook their heads at them in a most menacing way. But the knights caught them in their nets and slew them.

After this there came upon them a great multitude of swine, all of amazing size, with tusks a cubit long. With them there came wild men and women who had six hands each. But Alexander and his knights caught them in their nets and slew many of them.

Alexander and his host were greatly discomfited by all this, and Alexander ordered the men to build many fires outside the camp, around the lake. After this there came upon them a wondrous great beast, larger and stranger than an elephant, with three long horns on his forehead. He was in shape like a horse, and black in colour. This beast was called in the language of India 'Anddontrucion'. Before he went to the water to drink, he attacked the army. But Alexander went here and there among the troops and comforted them. This beast slew 28 of his knights and 52 of the others; but at last it fell into the nets and was slain.

After this there came out of the reeds a great multitude of mice, as big as foxes, and ate up the dead bodies. There was no living thing but died as soon as they bit it; but they did no harm to the troops.

Then there came flying among them bats, larger than wild doves, with teeth like those of men. They caused a lot of trouble and wounded many of the men: in some cases they bit off their noses, in other cases their ears.

In the early morning there came many birds as large as vultures, red in colour, with black feet and beaks. But they did no harm to the troops, but went to the lake side and drew fishes and eels out of the water, and ate them.

Then Alexander left these perilous places and came with his host to the country of Bactrice . . .

(ii) From 'KYNG ALISAUNDRE'
(B–text 6774–6994; modernised by RS)

The Trees of the Sun and Moon

The king by counsel of his best
Dight him hitherward in haste
And sent with Porus all his men
Into the city of Faacen.
But forty thousand with him he took,
As we finden in the book.
Alisaunder so rideth and wendeth
That he is comen the trowes ende [to the end of the trees]
The nutmeg and the setewale
On him smelleth, and the galingale;
The caneil and the liquorice   [cinnamon]
Sweet flavour giveth, I-wis,
The gillyflower, quybibbe and mace,
Ginger, cumin, gave odour of grace,
And under sun of alle spice
They hadden savour with delice.
That land was holy, he understood.
They alighted from their destreres good   [war-horses]
And went on foot, and many they met.
Every other faire grette.   [greeted them]
Of lions and pantheren
All their weeds, certes, weren   [clothes]
Haveth they no will to spin –
Their clothes been of beastes' skin.
Of the kinges come hath sonde   [messengers]
He greeted him and went to the king again.
Hear now of a wondrous man!
The bishop hight Longys, surely;
He was both black and grisly,
And rough and shouldered also.
His one foot was more than the other two.
He had boars' tusks and a wide mouth.

The king of him had selcouth.   [was scared of him]
He had of length ten great feet.
In a lion's skin he was y-shred;   [clad]
Of a beast that hight panther
His hood was, and hung about his swere.   [neck]
The king well fair there he greet
As soon as he him met,
And the king him said, by good reason
Of his coming thenchesoun.   [thither]
What helpeth it all to tell?
The bishop granted all his will,
And shriveth him and all tho[se]
That would with him to the trees go.
Now is the sun y-gone under.
The bishop leadeth the king to this wonder,
And three thousand knights him myde   [with him]
To the trees after yede.   [went]
Ne saw he never so fair atoure   [surroundings]
Nor smelled so sweet odour.
At the tree of the sun
Their sacrifice he begun.
The bishop to the king said
And to all his fellow-rede   [company]
'King,' he said, 'this tree honest
Asketh offering of no beast,
Neither of brooches nor of rings,
Nor of the mouth's cryings.
But in thine heart think all thy will,
And thou it shalt wite snell.   [know quickly]
For behold! upright thy steven   [cry]
Is y-heard in heaven.
The king saw a light like fire-brand
From the tree up to heaven stand.
At once on his knees he fell
Down there with his knights all,
And thought if he should the world win forth,
East and west, south and north,

If he should to Greece again wend
To see his mother and his friend[s].
The tree him answered again
In language of Indien:
'King Alisaunder, I tell thee cert,
Of all the world the third part
Thou shalt win and be of [it] king.
And wondrous worthy thine ending.
Hear my language, understand!
Ne comest thou never in Greece land;
Mother nor sister, nor thy kin
Ne shalt thou more in Greece seen.
Ere thou wast in thy begetting,
Of gods it was thy destining.
For all the world, I say to thee,
Otherwise it might not be.'
When the king heard this
For grief he changed colour, I-wis;
Woe was him for that answer
And that it had foretold so fell.
Then those men might have seen enough
Dukes and barons fall in a swoon.
Then flowed their tears, less and more,
Hands raised to pray and weeping sore
And they bewailed his prowess,
His youth, his strength and his largesse.
The king began to sigh full sore,
And bade them silence, less and more.
He comforted them and bade be still –
He must needs suffer God's will.
He called them great and worthy nobles;
They should accept and be at peace.
He took the bishop then aside,
For it was after the mid-night,
And they went right soon
To the tree of the moon.
Three knights he made with him go,

Of his bravest, and no more,
They were Dytonas, Philotas and Perdicas;
There were no more or less.
The king and his knights knelt down, cert,
And thus he said in his heart:
'Tree fair, I bid thee,
By thy life that thou tell me
When I shall die, in good fay   [faith]
Where and in which country?'
The tree him answered in Greek:
'Thou shalt die in Babylon,
Through envy and by treasons
Before all thy barons.
In the next year hereafterward
Thou shalt suffer death well hard!'
Then wept the king and his y-fere   [companions]
And made most rueful cheer.
His wits he forgot for sorrow
And went to lie down till the morrow.
His knights of Greece and Perse
Woe and sorrow began to rehearse,
They wept, and their clothes they tore;
No one ever saw such great care.
Philotas then to the king came,
And spoke to him in all their name.
'Sir,' he said, 'Understand!
We are with thee in a strange land.
It is not that all our friends
Are now with us at hand.
We have all many a private foe
That would gladly harm us too,
And wish deeply to grieve us;
But thou, make thyself vigorous.
What thou heardest is faerie –
Has thou not heart and flesh hardy?
Let be, sir, with such mourning,
And go comfort thy men.'

King Alisaunder, though he was woe,
Then took good heart him to.
Up he rose, and to his people goeth,
Makes them blithe, and nothing wroth,
Eateth and drinketh, playeth and laughs
As if he thought nothing thereof.
For he made him blithe and light,
Much joy made his knight[s].
All was forgot of sorrow and care –
That day he let forth fare.
Then it was eftsoons night,   [soon]
the king come to the bishop right,
And said he had forget
The thing that he would wyte   [know]
And the third time to him said
He should him to the tree lead
That was called that of the Sun,
For there was more he fain would con.   [learn]
The bishop granted him his will
And led him thither, silent still.
No creature with them was
But the true Perdicas.
And when he came unto the tree,
He fell right down upon his knee,
And thought thus, in great fay: [faith]
'Tree, I bid you to me say
When I shall hence depart,
And who shall my betrayer be?'
The tree answered with great ire:
'Parfay! thou art a wondrous sir,
And askest things without excuse.
Now is the time of April –
Thou shalt live all this year,
But not without great care.
Thou shalt all well overcome.
Thy ending shall take place
In the next year, as I describe,

The four and twentieth day of March.
Thou shalt death by poison suffer.
Thy traitor shall be captured.
But thou mayst not know thy foe,
For Clotho, Lachesis and Antropo,
The sisters, [Fates] hide it from thee.
No more, I tell thee, ask thou me!
Go out of our wood snell   [quickly]
For no more will I thee tell.'
When the king this admonition heard,
Quickly thence he fared
And, as we findeth in the book,
Of the bishop his leave he took,
For he knew his fated day.
He will find, if he may,
Though it be to him foredoomed,
In some manner to escape.
He went unto his host honest
And maketh him a rich feast,
And crieth loud and makes his cry,
No man shall believe that faerie,
But everyone shall simply laugh,
For he telleth no tale thereof.
Then thou mightest in many wise
Have seen solace and game arise,
Laughing, singing, and dancing made,
Stories told and riddles cracked.
Such chance the world keepeth –
Now man laugheth, now he weepeth.
Now man is hale, now he is sick;
There is no day to another alike.
No man that lives can borrow
From evening life until tomorrow.
April gives merry showers;
the birds sing, and spring the flowers.
Many obstacles are in love;
Steadfast seldom are lechers.

Hot love often after will go sour.
A fair jewel is a good neighbour.
The best thing is God to honour.

(iii) From 'THE BOOK OF SIR JOHN MANDEVILLE'

Of the goodness of the isle of Brahmins.
Of King Alexander. And wherefore the
Emperor of Ind is cleped Prester John

And beyond that isle is another isle great and good and
plenteous, where that be good folk and true and of good living
after their belief and of good faith. And albeit that they be not
christened nor have no perfect law, yet natheless of kindly law
they be full of all virtue. And they eschew all vices and all
malices and all sins, for they be not proud, nor covetous, nor
envious, nor wrathful, nor gluttons, nor lecherous, nor they do
to no man otherwise than they would that other men did to
them. And in this point they fulfil the ten commandments of
God, and give no charge of *avoir* nor of riches. And they lie not
nor they swear not for no occasion, but they say simply yea and
nay. For they say he that sweareth will deceive his neighbour,
and therefore all that they do they do without oath.

And men clepe that isle the isle of Brahmins, and some men
clepe it the land of faith. And through that land runneth a great
river that is cleped Tiberoboam. And in general all the men of
those isles and of all the marches thereabout be more true than
in any other countries thereabout, and more rightful than other
in all things.

In that isle is no thief nor murderer nor common woman nor
poor beggar, nor never was man slain in that country. And they
be so chaste and lead so good life as that they were religious
men. And they fast all days. And because they be so true and so
rightful and so full of all good conditions, they were never
grieved with tempests nor with thunder nor with leit nor with
hail nor with pestilence nor with war nor with hunger nor with
no other tribulation as we be many times amongst us for our

sins. Wherefore it seemeth well that God loveth them and is pleased with their creance for their good deeds.

They believe well in God that made all things, and Him they worship. And they prize no earthly riches, and so they be all rightful. And they live full ordinately and so soberly in meat and drink that they live right long, and the most part of them die without sickness when nature faileth them for eld.

And it befell in King Alexander's time that he purposed him to conquer that isle and to make them to hold of him. And when they of the country heard it, they sent messengers to him with letters that said thus: 'What may be enough to that man to whom all the world is sufficient? Thou shalt find nothing in us that may cause thee to war against us, for we have no riches nor none we covet, and all the goods of our country be in common. Our meat that we sustain withal our bodies is our riches. And instead of treasure of gold and silver we make our treasure of accord and peace and for to love every man other. And for to apparel with our bodies, we use a silly little clout for to wrap in our carrion. Our wives ne be not arrayed for to make no man pleasure but only convenable array for to eschew folly. When men pain them to array the body for to make it seem fairer than God made it, they do great sin, for man should not devise nor ask greater beauty than God hath ordained man to be at his birth. The earth ministereth to us two things, our livelihood that cometh of the earth that we live by, and our sepulchre after our death. We have been in perpetual peace till now that thou come to disinherit us. And also we have a king not for to do justice to every man, for he shall find no forfeit among us, but for to keep noblesse and for to show that we be obedient we have a king. For justice ne hath not among us no place, for we do to no man otherwise than we desire that men do to us, so that rightwiseness nor vengeance have nought to do amongst us, so that nothing that thou may take from us but our good peace, that always hath dured among us.'

And when King Alexander had read these letters, he thought that he should do great sin for to trouble them. And then he sent them sureties that they should not be afraid of him, and that they should keep their good manners and their good peace as they had used before of custom. And so he let them alone.

Another isle there is that men clepe Oxydraces and another isle that men clepe Gymnosophistae, where there is also good folk and full of good faith. And they hold for the most part the good conditions and customs and good manners as men of the country abovesaid. But they go all naked.

Into that isle entered King Alexander to see the manner. And when he saw their great faith and their truth that was amongst them, he said that he would not grieve them, and bade them ask of him what that they would have of him, riches or anything else, and they should have it with good will.

And they answered that he was rich enough that had meat and drink to sustain the body with, for the riches of this world that is transitory is not worth. But if it were in his power to make them immortal, thereof would they pray him and thank him. And Alexander answered them that it was not in his power to do it because he was mortal as they were.

And then they asked him why he was so proud and so fierce and so busy for to put all the world under his subjection, 'right as thou were a god and hast no term of thy life, neither day nor hour; and willest to have all the world at thy commandment, that shall leave thee without fail ere thou leave it. And right as it hath been to other men before thee, right so it shall be to other after thee. And from hence shalt thou bear nothing. But as thou were born naked, right so all naked shall thy body be turned into earth that thou were made of. Wherefore thou shouldst think and impress it in thy mind that nothing is immortal but only God that made all thing.'

By the which answer Alexander was greatly astonished and abashed and all confused departed from them.

(iv) From THE ALLITERATIVE 'ALEXANDER B' (ed. W. W. Skeat, EETS extra series 31 (1878); translated into English prose by RS)

How King Dindimus sent letters to King Alexander

The dear King Dindimus, the doctor of wisdom, whom the Brahmans revere as king of their land, sent loving letters to King Alexander, the highest of princes, who had become the most formidable and greatest of kings, and wrote to his people with gracious greetings and wishes for their happiness:

By your message, man, that you sent to me, and when we saw the sand imprinted by your sole, we recognised your desire and eagerness to learn of the true wisdom that belongs to us. I know that you wish to learn the best laws and lore: right wisdom is worth all the world's riches. There was never an emperor on earth who was able to rule his inferiors without wisdom; if there were, the lowest of his subjects could outdo him and deal with him as with a witless fool.

None the less, lord king, I warn you now, it seems impossible to our ascetic race that you should be able to endure our ways, or last any time in the life that we lead. Our life and our laws are not like yours, and we abhor all wickedness in our hearts. The deeds that you do are in discord with ours; and we do not revere the gods that you worship.

As for your request, lord king, to tell the truth about our way of life in brief, I pray you in your graciousness to excuse us, for we cannot describe to you all of our customs. Even if I send you these letters describing our life, it will profit us nothing to preach of our doings; for you have no time to attend to my instruction, busy as you are with making war. Yet you must not think that it is through apathy that I am unwilling to tell you about our life; I will certainly tell you as much as I can think of.

We, poor Brahmans, brethren in God, lead a simple and pure life. We desire to have nothing else in this world but what will sustain our simple life. We put up with privation and endure poverty; we think it necessary to take only so much as will leave no waste. It is no part of our law to wound the land with sharp ploughshares and to shape furrows. We do not turn the soil of the fields, and we sow no seed, nor do we plough up the ground with oxen. We do not sail onto the sea with nets to make our food of the finny fishes. We never go hunting or hawking, and make no prey of four-footed beasts; nor do we go into the meadows with stealth to entrap the birds of heaven. When we wish to eat we make no complaint; we have so much at hand that we require no more. We make no effort to acquire other goods, and have no desire of dainties except what our mother may bring forth for us – I mean the earth, whom we regard as our kin. She gives us the nourishment we need, and sends us at once, without sweat or labour, whatever we want.

None of those who live in our land want to take more than their due measure, and as a result we are always strong and never sick, and maintain our health till we pass from hence. Our people are devoted to God; they love him as their lord and like to serve him, unlike many other folk who fill their bellies and take more than they need. We make no medicine, and no man needs to pray for the healing of his body. We have assigned to us a certain sum of years, after which we shall lose our lives and cease to continue; and we can tell when our time falls due. One man may live a little longer than another: the king of heaven in his kindness leaves us in doubt when the day of death will come. It is the nature of our kind that when our bodies wear out, when our limbs fail and our heat lessens, then we shall leave behind our life, while our soul shall journey to bliss with him that shaped us. No matter what cold comes upon us, we use no fire to warm our fingers; we are whole of body and death is no evil.

We always flee from fleshly lusts. We practise meekness. All manner of things that might soil us with sin cease before long.

I advise you, wealthy and powerful as you are, to hasten to overcome those enemies that are within you. If you could conquer the foes that dwell in your flesh, no outward enemy could harm you. But you fight instead against the foes that are outside you, and carry with you all that are within. We, if we spy any enemies within us, we struggle without sleep or sloth until we have slain them; and because we overcome all those that are within us, we have no fear of foes that are without. We take no trouble to go against them, and we do not seek the help of any man under heaven. We fear no man and have no wish to conquer any one on water or on land.

We cover our bodies with the boughs of trees, and we have fruit for food at need. We have much milk among our people, and so have no lack of wholesome food.

(v) From JOHN GOWER, *Confessio Amantis*

The king of Bragman Dindimus
Wrote unto Alisaundre thus
In blaminge of the Grekes feith
And of the misbeleve he saith,
How they for every membre hadden
A sondry god, to whom they spradden
Her armes and of help besoughten.

Minerve for the hede they soughten,
For she was wise, and of a man
The wit and reson which he can
Is in the celles of the brain,
Wherof they made her soverain.

Mercurie, which was in his dawes
A great speker of false lawes,
On him the keping of the tunge
They laiden, whan they speke or sunge.

For Bachus was a gloton eke
Him for the throte they beseke,
That he it wolde washen ofte
With suote drinkes and with softe.

The god of shulders and of armes
Was Hercules, for he in armes
The mightiest was to fight,
To him tho limmes they behight.
The god whom that they clepen Mart
The brest to kepe hath for his part,
For with the herte in his ymage

That he addresse to his corage.
And of the galle the goddesse,
For she was ful of hastinesse,
Of wrath and light to greve also,
They made and said, it was Juno.

Cupide, which the brond of fire
Bare in his hond, he was the fire
Of the stomack, which boileth ever,
Wherof the lustes ben the lever.

To the goddesse Cereres,
Whiche of the corn yaf her encres,
Upon the feith that tho was take
The wombes cure was betake.

And Venus through the lechery,
For whiche they her deify,
She kepte all down the remenaunt
To thilke office appertenaunt.

(vi) From THE UPRIGHT LIVES OF THE HEATHENS
BRIEFLY NOTED:
or, Epistles and Discourses betwixt Alexander the Conqueror
and Dindimus King of the Brachmans' (1683)

1 *Dindimus, King of the Brachmans, his letter to
Alexander the Conqueror*

King, we have heard of thy battles and victories, but what shall
suffice thee whom all the world sufficeth not? Riches we have
none for thee: why then shouldst thou war on us? All our goods
are to common us: vile things and scarce we have, instead of
gold and great array: our women are not arrayed to please, for
great array is counted nought with us; not highness nor fairness:
our women desire no more fairness than they have by kind; dry
ditches and dens stand us in double stead, for harbour while we
live, and for graves when we are dead. If we have sometimes a
king, it is not to do us right; for honesty by kind will do that:
we have amongst us neither doom nor plea, for we do nothing

that needs redress, either by doom or plea: we desire no more than reason and kind asketh; we hold that needful which we know is measurable: our people have one law, and do nothing against this law of kind: we use no trade to make us covetous: we shun and forsake sloth and lechery. We do nothing that needs punishment. It is unlawful for us to wound the hills with coulters, or the ax: we use no glutting or outrageousness of meat or drink; therefore we be not sick: we dwell in the dry ditches; heaven finds us a covering, the earth a lodging: we be not warriors, we make peace with good living, not with strength. We seek not plenteous gain; for it is right liking to us to behold the firmament and stars of heaven: we be men of single speech, it's common to us all not to lie. The God of all grace is our god, for he hath liking in our words and deeds, by our manner of speaking; he is a word, a spirit, love and thought, and is not pleased with worldly riches, but with holy works and thanks for his grace.

Upon this King Alexander answered with taunts and jeers, as if Dindimus despised God's benefits, counting all handicrafts sinful; and [four words obliterated] are gods, and so have envy to God, and blame his fairest creatures.

But Dindimus answered, We be not at home in this world, come not to dwell here, &c. We be not aliond [?] with charges of sin, but without each manner of charge, we draw near to our own houses, and lie fast homewards; we say not, we be gods, but we say, we will not abuse the goodness of God Almighty: we say, things are seemly which are lawful; God hath put the use of things into men's freedom; then he that leaveth, and followeth the best, is not God, but is made God's friend. When ye swell in wealth, and pride hath blown you up, ye forget that ye are men, and say that God reckons of mankind. Ye build temples to your selves, in which ye shed men's blood; and therefore I call you wood (or mad) for ye wot not what ye do; and if ye despise God's writing, then ye hold in the sacrilege.

Then Alexander writeth this epistle to him again, with many taunts and jeers, comparing them in their sacrifices to them that were in prison, saying, The cause why they tilled not the ground was because they had no iron: and their women not costly arrayed, is no marvel, because they have not wherewith.

Dindimus answered, Ye make wars and battles, and war outwardly against men, because ye have not overcome the enemy within; but we Brachmans have overcome the inward battles in our members, and rest secure, and have no battles outwardly; we behold the firmament of heaven, her birds singing; we be healed and fed with leaves and fruits of trees; we drink water, and sing songs in worship of God, and take heed, and think of the life coming. We be approved with few words, and even still and hold our peace. Ye say what shall be done, and yet do it not: your wit and wisdom is in your lips; ye hunger after gold, ye need houses and servants, ye want reverence and worship.

11 *Of the ambassadors sent by Alexander to Dindimus, with his reply to them*

After that, Alexander sent ambassadors to Dindimus, requiring him, and charging him, to come to him without delay; promising him great gifts and rewards if he obeyed, which if he did not he should lose his life; and all this in the name of Alexander, the king of all men, and son of the great God Jupiter.

But Dindimus singling at this vapour, and not moving his head from the leaves he lay upon, and lay still, and answered after this manner, Soth fast, God the great king giveth man right, and doth no man wrong; he never begot injury, but light, life, peace, the water, body and souls, which he also receives when they have finished their course; nor was he ever the author of lust. This is my Lord and only God, who as he hates murder, so he wageth not war, nor raiseth strife. The things I seek, I easily attain to; those things which I regard not, I am not to be driven to; if therefore Alexander take my head, and slay me, he shall not destroy my soul, which will return to the Lord, while the body which was taken out of the earth shall thereunto return; for I being made a spirit, shall ascend unto my God, who included us in the flesh, and placed us upon this earth, to try us,

whether we being gone forth from him, would live unto him, as
he hath commanded, who demandeth an account of those that
depart; for he is a judge of all injuries: and the sighs of those
that are injuriously treated, become the pain of those that injure
them. Let Alexander therefore threaten them that love silver and
gold, and fear death; neither of which have place amongst the
Brachmans, who do neither fear the one nor love the other. Go
therefore and tell Alexander, Dindimus wants him not, and if he
wants Dindimus, let him come to him.

III *The conference between Alexander and Dindimus*

Which being reported to Alexander, he was the more desirous
to see the single old man, that could conquer him after he had
conquered so many nations, and so left all pomp and boasting,
comes to him, and said, I come to hear a word of wisdom from
thee, whom I hear dost converse with God.

To whom Dindimus replied, Why disturbest thou our peace?
Very willingly would I administer to thee the words of the
wisdom of God, hadst thou but place in thy mind to receive the
gift of God administered; but thy mind being filled with various
lusts, unsatiable avarice, and devilish desire to rule, which fight
against me and my designs of drawing thee off from destroying
nations, and shedding human blood, are in all things contrary
to the wisdom by which I and the Brachmans are led, who
worship God, love men, contemn gold, despise death and slight
pleasures, whereas Alexander and his fear death, love gold,
covet pleasure, hate men and despise God; adding, How can I
speak unto thee the words of the wisdom of God, whose
cogitations are so filled with pomp, ostentation and inordinate
lust, that a whole world is not able to satiate thee? How then
shall I suffice thee? And further, God hath made thee little, and
thou desirest all the world; yet needest thou have as little land
at last, as thou seest me lie upon, or thy self sit upon: If thou
learnest wisdom of me, it is all thou shalt have, etc. I know
God's secrets; for God doth will that I be partaker of his works;
then whether, sayst thou, is most right, to misbid men, or to

defend them and do them right? To shed and kill, or to keep and save? If thou slay me, I go to God.

However, he refused not to give Alexander that counsel, which as he confessed, was convinced in his heart, was good, but could not follow, viz. to cease warring against men without, and engage himself in another warfare, against the enemies within himself, his lusts, affections and desires, if he desired to be rich indeed, and to be a true victor; assuring him, that all his power, all his hosts, all his riches, all his pomp, would at last not avail him any thing; but (saith he) if thou wilt hearken unto my words, thou shalt possess of my goods, who have God to my friend, and whose inspiration I enjoy within me——Thus shalt thou overcome lust, the mother of penury, which never obtains what it seeks; thus thou shalt with us honour thy self, by becoming such as God had created thee. Adding, though thou slay me for telling thee these profitable things, I fear not; for (saith he) I shall return to my God, who created all things, who knows my cause, and before whom nothing is hidden. I know not, saith he, whether thou shalt be so happy as to find thy self persuaded by my words, but I assure thee, if thou be not, when thou art departed hence, I shall see thee punished for thy actions, and hear thee lament with deep and sharp sighs the misery thou has put many to, etc, viz. when thou shalt have no other companion than the memory of the evils thou has heaped upon thyself; for, saith he, I know the pains justly inflicted by God upon unjust men. Then thou shalt say unto me, Dindimus, how good a counsellor wert thou to me, etc!

These things Alexander heard (as it's said of Herod concerning John Baptist) not only without wroth, but with a placid countenance, and replied, O Dindimus! thou true teacher of the Brachmans, thou comest of God, I have found thee the most excellent amongst men, by reason of the spirit that is in thee: I know all thou hast spoken is true; God hath brought thee forth, and sent thee into this place, in which thou art happy and rich, wanting nothing, enjoying much rest and peace. But what shall I do, who cohabit with continual slaughter? I live in great dread, and am afraid of my own warders; I dread more my friends than my enemies; I may not leave them and trust others. At days I grieve other men, and am at night grieved myself: if I would live in the desert, my lieutenants would not suffer me; and though they would, being in this state, it is not lawful for me to quit them; for how shall I defend my self before God, who hath assigned me this lot? But thou reverend old man, and servant of God, for these words of wisdom, wherewith thou hast helped and rejoiced me, dehorting me from war, receive thou my presents, and despise me not; I am affected with kindness, honouring wisdom. And so commanded his servants to bring forth gold and silver, bread and oil, and several sorts of array; which Dindimus beholding, laughed, saying to Alexander, Persuade (if thou canst) the birds about the woods to receive thy gold, or sing the better for it; but if thou canst not persuade them, nor shalt thou ever persuade me to be worse than they; I therefore receive no unprofitable present, which I can neither eat nor drink; nor do I serve soul-hurtful riches etc. Here is nothing in this desert to be bought with gold, for God gives me all things freely, etc, selling nothing for gold, but freely bestowing all good things, and even the mind on those that freely accept it, etc. But for that I will not grieve thee too much, I will receive the oil of thee; and he walking about the wood gathered some sticks, and kindled a fire, he said, the Brachmans have all things, being fed by Providence; and into the fire he poured the oil, till it was all consumed, and sang a hymn to God Almighty, as followeth:

'O God Immortal! I give thee in all things thanks; for thou rulest in all things; giving all things abundantly to thy creatures for their food. Thou creating this world, dost preserve it, expecting the souls which thou hast sent into it, that thou mayst, as God, justify those that have led a pious life, and condemn those that have not obeyed thy laws; for all righteous judgement is with thee, and life eternal prepared by thee, who with eternal goodness showest mercy unto all.'

Lastly, now as concerning the Brachmans of India, Suidas[1] tells of one Brachman that prescribed their rites and laws, etc.

Of the Indian philosophers, or men learned and religious, the

Brachmans obtain the first place, as being nearest in sect to the Greeks. They are, after their manner, Nazarites from the womb: so soon as their mother is conceived of them, there are learned men appointed, which come to the mother with songs, containing precepts of chastity: As they grow in years, they change their masters; they have their places of exercise in a grove, nigh to the city, where they are busied in grave concerns: They eat no living creatures, nor have use of women, live frugally, and lie upon skins; they will instruct such as will hear them, but their hearers must neither sneeze, spit nor speak. When they have in this strict course spent 37 years, they may live more at pleasure and liberty, in diet, habit, proper habitations, and the use of gold and marriage; they conceal their mysteries from their wives, lest they should blab them abroad: They esteem this life as man's conception, but his death day to be his birthday unto that true and happy life, to him which hath been rightly religious, (a worthy sentence!). The Brachmans hold the world to be created corruptible, round, ruled by the high God. Water they imagine to have been the beginning of making the world; and that besides the four elements there is a fifth nature, whereof the heavens and stars consist: They hold the immortality of the soul, and of the torments of hell, and that the souls of the righteous go to God.

Megasthenes[2] commendeth Mandanis (one of the Brachmans) saying, that when Alexander's messengers told him, that he must come to the son of Jupiter, with promise of rewards if he came, but if otherwise, menacing torture. He answered, that neither was he Jupiter's son, nor did possess any great part of the earth. As for himself, he neither respected his gifts nor feared his threatenings; for while he lived, India yielded him sufficient; if he died, he would be freed from age, and exchange for a better and purer life: whereupon Alexander both pardoned and praised him.

Clemens Alexandrinus[3] speaks of their fastings, and other austere courses, out of Alex. Polyhist[or] De rebus judicis, 'The Brachmans (saith he) neither eat any quick thing, nor drink wine, but some of them eat every day, as we do; some only every third day: They contemn death, nor much esteem life, believing to be born again.' Clem. Alex. *Strom*. 1.3.

Suidas tells of a nation called Brachmans, inhabiting an island in the sea, where Alexander erected a pillar, with inscription, that he had passed so far. They live an hundred and fifty years, and have neither bread, wine, flesh, metal nor houses, but live of the fruits and clear water, and are very religious, etc. They slay no beasts in sacrifice, but affirm that God accepteth unbloody sacrifices of prayer, and more delighteth in man his own image.

To Alexander did the Indian Magi (so doth Arrianus[4] call their Brachmans) say, that he was but as other men, saving that he had less rest, and more troublesome, and being dead should enjoy no more land than would serve to cover his body; and every man (said they) stamping with their feet on the ground, hath as much as he treadeth on. Arrian. lib.7.

Eusebius[5] writeth out of Bradsanes Cyrus,[6] that amongst the Indians and Bactrians were many thousand Brachmans, which as well by tradition as by law worshipped no image, nor ate any quick creature, drank no wine nor beer, only attending on divine things; whereas the other Indians are very vicious, yea, some hunt men, sacrifice and devour them, and were as idolaters. Euseb. *depres. Evang. lib.6 cap. 8.*

Heurnius[7] reporteth, that they have books and prophets, which they allege for confirmation of their opinions; and that they have in their writings the decalogue, with the explication thereof; that they adjure all of their society to silence, touching their mysteries; and that they adore the God which created heaven and earth, often repeating the sentence, I adore thee, O God, with thy grace and aid forever. When they wash themselves (which is often) they lay a little ashes on their foreheads and breasts, saying, that they shall return unto ashes. Heur. *indic. cap. 3.*

There was a Malabar poet, which wrote nine hundred epistles against their pago-gods, each consisting of eight verses, wherein he speaks many things elegantly of the divine providence of heaven, and the torments of hell, and other things, agreeing to the Christian faith, that God is present everywhere, and give to everyone according to his estate; that celestial blessedness consists in the vision of God; that the damned in Hell shall be tormented millions of years in flames, and shall never die.

Aristotle[8] in his *Ethick*, lib. 10. cap.4.7, said, they that did these things did them not as men, but as having something divine, or of God in them.

Those that desire to read more of their divinity, philosophy, and manner of living, are referred to a paper lately published entitled, A Dialogue betwixt an East Indian Brachman, and a Christian, price 1d.

(vii) From GILBERT HAY, 'THE BUIK OF ALEXANDER' (modernised by RS)

Alexander visits Paradise

When they come near that they the place might see,
It was so huge, marvellous and high,
And also was so pleasant and so fair,
So temperate and so sober was the air,
And where before was woods and wilderness,
Nothing but fruit and flowers and spices was;
The crags ran all along the river's sides,
The trees of balm that glittered gold o'erhead,
The flowers blossomed fairly in the field,
The crags were fashioned out of solid gold;
There was no cloud nor motion in the air,
But soft and sweet the weather was, and fair.
That place to see, they took so great delight
That from their selves they were so ravished quite
That of no earthly thing they took no care
But all his servants soundly fell asleep.

The way was wide, the walls were very high,
That scarcely to the top a man might see;
The passage through the which the flood came down

Was like a postern of a walléd town,
But it was muckle, and of great quantity,
And where it fell, it was like to the sea.
The river, that was broad and deep and clear,
Was never more fair, not in well nor river;
It stood as deep as a loch, and ran not fast,
Right from the place that in the ship he passed.
They saw no other gate, postern nor entry,
But kirnels [battlements] on the wall that was so high.
Then was he more abashed than before,
For though he had of ladders twenty score,
And coupled all together in a line,
They could not reach up to the kirnelling.
You would not know that there was any night,
For ever as day the sun was fair and bright.
The king was not in royal habit there,
But as a send [messenger] of Alexander he was;
Inside his ship three days long there he lay,
Ever in prayers, both by night and day,
For he knew well it was not in his power
To get an answer from that holy place,
Nor find the way to pass up to that height,
But if it were through grace of God almighty.

Then slept he, as all mankind may do,
And in his sleep God Ammon came him to,
And bade him draw his ship to the walls near,
And hold him in devotion and prayer,
And ask that they would tribute to him bring
Of Paradise, for Alexander the king,
And taught him in what kind of language
That he should ask for tribute and obeisance,
And bade him say his master was not here,
But Ptolemy, who was his messenger.
The king awoke, and did as he him bade,
And soon the ship along the wall was laid.
The king went on his knees in prayer,

The water rose up to the kirnelling,
And bore the ship up to the wall so high.
(He had put forth Dauclyne and Ptolemy,
And in the ship they left him quite alone;
And in this way he to the wall is gone.)
And when he was uplifted in the air,
Then he beheld the region that was fair,
And all the country backward to the west;
And in the sea one side his sight he cast,
And saw the golden crag that stood it by,
Of massy gold, shining so gloriously;
He saw the circle of Paradise about,
Which closed is all with sea, without a doubt,
All but one thread that answers to the land
Where that the four rivers are flowing out.
The walls were rough and covered all with green,
With spice and balms and gold shining between;
He saw the four floods which all flowing were
Out of that place, and shall do evermore –
Each one seemed from the other leagues ten,
And from the mountain flowed each in its glen;
Betwixt the floods were fruit and flowers fair,
But earthly men there might none there repair,
The land so straight was rising up so high,
And of wild beast so huge a quantity,
That none might find a way to come or go,
But he that through the will of God comes so.

The place within is mickle and spacious,
And all the land about so gracious,
So pleasant and delectable for to see,
Suppose a man there twenty year should be,
He would not think it twenty dayés long,
For such a melody of birdés sang,
With all pleasance that mankind's wit might think,
That they list not for other meat and drink,
But when that they three dayés there had been,

They thought they had but come in yestereen.
Then Alexander in spirit so ravished was,
He would right fain have been within the place,
But that would never be, of no kind wise;
So at the last he called in twice or thrice,
And askéd tribute to the emperor
Which of this whole earth is the conqueror.
With that, an angel to the wall did come,
Said, 'Alexander, here art thou right welcome.
For thy tribute an apple here I give;
And think that thou hast short time for to live,
And keep it well, when thou comest home, it weigh:
It shall turn hue what time that thou be fey.
Thou shalt neither come into this place, nor look;
Farewell', he said; with that his leave he took.

The water waned, the ship sank slowly down;
He wakened up his men, and made them move.
They passéd down withouten more ado
Unto the place where that the ship was made.
They left the ship and took then to the land
– Then three months they had been on that errand –
And soon to the mainland they came again,
Of which the lords were right impressed with wonder,
Saying, 'Welcome, our lord and governor –
Now we may say thou art full emperor
Of all this earth, since we have certain knowledge
That Paradise hath yielded thee its homage.'

NOTES

ALEXANDER'S LETTER TO ARISTOTLE ABOUT INDIA

1 334 BC. The Granicus is a small river in the Troad.

2 Fasiace is a Greek version of the Sanskrit word *prachyaka*, 'the eastern realm'. Porus's kingdom was centred on the upper Punjab, southeast of modern Rawalpindi.

3 This description is borrowed from that of the palace of the kings of Persia, Herodotus 7.27.2. There is a similar description in the Greek Alexander Romance 3.28.

4 The Caspian Gates was the name normally given in antiquity to a defile in the Elburz Mountains near Rey. However, it also became attached to the Derbend Pass in the Caucasus; and because the Paropamisus or Hindu Kush was also sometimes known as Caucasus in antiquity, the Caspian Gates were in the Alexander legend placed further east and treated as the gateway to the world of fabulous creatures. See R. Stoneman, 'Romantic ethnography: Central Asia and India in the *Alexander Romance*', *Ancient World* (1994).

5 This belief about the origins of silk is first mentioned in Virgil, *Georgics* 2.121. Silkworms (and hence the truth about silk) were first smuggled out of China in the reign of Justinian (527–65).

6 This charismatic act of leadership is recounted by Arrian, *Anab* 6.26. It actually took place in the Gedrosian Desert (southeast Iran).

7 Ctesias *FGrH* 688 F 45.14.

8 A mistake for *veratrum*. The explanation is taken from Isidore, *Etymologiae* 17.9.24.

9 This curious sentence is not in the earlier Latin version. It apparently rests on a confusion of hippopotami with hippocentauri: cf. Isid. *Etym.* 11.3.39.

10 The earlier Latin text here includes 'spotted lynxes, tigers and shaggy panthers'.

11 An unidentified monster which regularly occurs in the accounts of Alexander's Indian adventures. Cf. the note in my *The Greek Alexander Romance* (Harmondsworth: Penguin, 1991), 196, n. 137.

12 Called 'night-crows' in the earlier Latin version.

13 Dionysus was thought to have originated in Nysa in India. Alexander's soldiers thought they had found Nysa in a valley in Afghanistan (not certainly identified), where ivy grew as at home. (Ivy was the special plant of Dionysus.) Part of the ideology of Alexander's expedition was to follow in the footsteps of these explorer gods.

14 In antiquity the earth was thought to be surrounded by a river known as Ocean. The conception survived into the Middle Ages, as can be seen on medieval maps such as the Hereford Mappa Mundi. See, e.g., P. D. A. Harvey, *Medieval Maps* (London: British Library, 1991).

15 This curious sentence is an addition by the author of the present Latin text.

16 The Fish-eaters were a tribe of South Arabia encountered by Alexander's army, and they seem to represent a surviving pocket of Neolithic culture. There may be confusion with another group of fish-eaters mentioned by Herodotus (1.20.2) on the river Araxes. The sentence in square brackets is only in the earlier Latin version.

17 The Dog-heads are a regular feature of the Central Asian landscape from Herodotus (4.191) onwards; cf. Ctesias *FGrH* 688 F 45.37 ff. See, in general, D. G. White, *Myths of the Dog-Man* (Chicago: Chicago University Press, 1991). The gloss is a quotation from Isidore, *Etymologiae* 11.3.15.

18 These trees also feature in Ctesias *FGrH* 688 F 45.17; Klaus Karttunen, *India in Early Greek Literature* (Helsinki: Finnish Oriental Society, 1989), 220.

19 Olympias was murdered in 316 BC by Cassander, who had become King of Macedonia.

20 This story of the valley of diamonds, famous from the story of Sinbad in the *Arabian Nights*, first appears in Pseudo-Epiphanius, *De Gemmis*.

21 The Latin expression is 'two or three congii'. A *congius* is about six pints.

22 *Sacros*: a mistake for *scaros*, 'parrot-fish'.

ON THE WONDERS OF THE EAST

1 The text is numbered here as in the edition of Claude Lecouteux, *De Rebus in Oriente Mirabilibus*. This differs from the order of chapters in the Latin text edited by Stanley Rypins, *Three Old English Prose Texts*. See further Introduction, p. 19.

2 This famous story goes back to Herodotus, 3.102–5. See Klaus Karttunen, *India in Early Greek Literature* (Helsinki: Finnish Oriental Society, 1989), 171–6.

FROM 'THE CHRONICLE OF GEORGE THE MONK'

1 Byzantium, which was founded by the legendary Byzas, and refounded by Constantine as New Rome (later Constantinople) in AD 324. Alexander had no connection with the city.

2 This is a version of the story in Josephus *AJ* 11.326–339

3 Daniel 8: 5–8, 21–2.

4 This story is also in Ps.-Hecataeus (Jacoby *FGrH* 264 F 21), reported in Josephus, *Against Apion* I. 201–4, where the archer is called Mosallamus.

5 The Battle of Issus, 333 BC.

6 The story of Candace is also in the Greek Alexander Romance, where she is Queen of Meroe (Ethiopia). Only Jewish tradition makes her engage in a sexual liaison with Alexander.

7 Alexander makes the same complaint in Plutarch, *de tranquillitate animi* 466D; cf. Val. Max. 8.14 ext.2.

8 Alexander's Pillars are shown on the late antique map known as the Tabula Peutingeriana with the note 'Quousque Alexander'.

9 These details are borrowed from Iambulus's Utopian account of the Long-lived people of India: Diod. Sic. 11.57.4.

10 See note 11 on the *Letter to Aristotle about India*.

11 This information seems to derive from Bardesanes' *Book of the Laws of Countries*.

PALLADIUS, 'ON THE LIFE OF THE BRAHMANS'

1 Genesis 2: 10–14. Paradise is envisaged as lying in the East, beyond the River of Ocean.

2 These pillars are shown on the late antique map known as the Tabula Peutingeriana.

3 In Ethiopia. Ethiopia and India were often confused in antiquity.

4 Sri Lanka.

5 The Indian Ocean, known in antiquity as the Red Sea.

6 The pygmies of South India are referred to already by Ctesias F. 45, 21 and 45f; cf. K. Karttunen, *India in Early Greek Literature* (Helsinki, 1989), 128f. They turn up also in the Greek Alexander Romance, 2.44.

7 That is, like monks.

8 For this description, cf. the Greek Alexander Romance 3.4ff., and Strabo 15.1.60, quoting Megasthenes.

9 In actual fact no part of India lies south of the equator. For vague ideas about the Antipodes in antiquity, cf. Pliny *Natural History* 4.12. 89–90, who remarks that 'some' place the Happy Land of the Hyperboreans between us and the Antipodes: this is seen as an appropriate location for a blessed race like that of the Brahmans.

10 See note 11 on the *Letter to Aristotle*.

11 Second century AD: the historian of Alexander.

12 Ca. 55–135, of Hierapolis. Reared as a slave, he was freed by his master Epaphroditus and became a distinguished Stoic teacher.

13 The address to Wisdom as a goddess may be a Gnostic touch: B. Berg, 'Dandamis: an early Christian portrait of Indian asceticism', *Classica et medievalia*, 31 (1970), 269–305 (279). Providence is regularly the ruler of the world in the Greek Alexander Romance.

14 An Indian 'philosopher' who attached himself to Alexander's expedition at Taxila, and on falling ill at Susa committed suicide by burning.

15 Sir John Marshall, the excavator of Taxila, wondered whether the name of this river is a recollection of the Tamra-nala at Taxila. The identification seems over-hopeful.

16 The same point is made in a Jewish legend about Alexander and King Kazia (Palestinian Talmud, *Baba Mezia* II.5.8c); see I. J. Kazis, *The Gests of Alexander of Macedon* (Cambridge, Mass.: Medieval Academy of America, 1962), 20–2.

17 *Amerimnia*, a word of similar sense to *ataraxia*, 'untroubledness', the keynote of the Cynic (and Epicurean) philosophies.

18 Onesicritus, a Cynic philosopher and contemporary historian of Alexander. See Truesdell S. Brown, *Onesicritus* (Berkeley, 1949); Lionel Pearson, *The Lost Histories of Alexander the Great* (Philadelphia, 1960), 83–113. The meeting of Onesicritus and the Brahmans is described in Strabo 15.1.63, following Onesicritus's own account.

19 Pataliputra, modern Patna, the capital of the Maurya Empire in the second century BC. The other names, except Mesopotamia, are nonsense names.

20 A Christian touch? It could also be derived from Hindu theology, which set aside a selection of 19 different hells for the sinner.

21 Alexander in actual fact was anxious to continue to eastern India, but was prevented by a mutiny of his troops.

22 A fascinating foreshadowing of Tolstoy's story, 'How much land does a man need?' The surviving portion of the Geneva papyrus (Introduction, p. xxi) begins at this point.

23 Brahmans in ancient India regularly performed a role as royal adviser.

24 The description seems to recall the Gospel parable of Dives and Lazarus.

25 A similar 'crisis of confidence' occurs in Alexander's 'mutability' speech in the Greek Alexander Romance (3.6).

26 The oil is the only one of these gifts which it is proper for a Brahman to accept, as is stated in the *Laws of Manu*.

27 The discourse on vegetarianism which follows here is quite a bit longer than can have been the case in the Geneva papyrus (the relevant columns are missing). A much more intelligent defence of vegetarianism is mounted by Porphyry in *De Abstinentia* IV.

28 This passage is an attack on the wild-beast shows of Imperial Rome.

29 The Macedonian devotion to heavy drinking was famous, but Dandamis seems to have an eye more on Roman orgies here.

30 Followers of Epicurus (341–270 BC), whose recipe for the happy life was maximisation of pleasure and minimisation of pain through simple living.

31 Called after the Stoa (portico) in Athens where the earliest Stoics taught. Stoics were not normally regarded as particularly acquisitive;

perhaps the allusion is to the very wealthy Roman Stoic philosopher Seneca.

ALEXANDER THE GREAT'S JOURNEY TO PARADISE

1 'And a river went out of Eden to water the garden; and from thence it was parted, and became into four heads ... Pison ... Gihon ... Hiddekel ... and Euphrates' (Genesis 2: 10–14). These rivers are usually identified as the Ganges, Nile, Tigris and Euphrates. Medieval maps show Paradise as an island, and the four rivers running out of that island, beneath the encircling Ocean, into the inhabited world.

2 The chief city of Persis and summer capital of the Persian Empire.

3 The legend is certainly of Jewish origin, first occurring in the Talmud (Tamid 32b); hence the prominence of the Jewish sage.

4 Proverbs 27: 20: 'Hell and destruction are never full; so the eyes of man are never satisfied.'

THE UPRIGHT LIVES OF THE HEATHENS BRIEFLY NOTED

1 Suidas: the Byzantine lexicon more correctly called the *Suda*.

2 Megasthenes: see Strabo 15.1.68.

3 Clement of Alexandria (c. 150–215): the reference is to *Stromateis* ('Miscellanies') 3.194. See J.W. McCrindle, *Ancient India as described in Classical Literature* (1901; repr. New Delhi 1979), 183–4. Alexander Polyhistor (105–after 49 BC): a historian of varied interests.

4 Arrian 7.1. 5–6.

5 Eusebius (ca. 260–340): *Praeparatio evangelica* 6.8.

6 Bradsanes: i.e., Bardesanes of Syria (Bardaisan of Edessa), author of the *Book of the Laws of Countries*.

7 O. Heurnius, *Barbaricae philosophiae antiquitates* (Leiden, 1600); the earliest of a flood of seventeenth-century Indology. Heurnius's work is characterised as 'trivial' by Wilhelm Halbfass, *India and Europe* (New York, 1988), 147.

8 Aristotle, *Nicomachean Ethics* 10.7, 1177a 13–17: 'Whether it be reason or something else that is this element which is thought to be our natural ruler and guide and to take thought of things noble and divine, whether it be itself also divine or only the most divine element in us, the activity of this in accordance with its proper virtue will be perfect happiness.' The statement is a general one and has nothing to do with Brahmans in Aristotle's text.

SUGGESTIONS FOR FURTHER READING

Barron, W. R. J., *Medieval English Romance*, London, 1987.

Bosworth, A. B., *Conquest and Empire: the Career of Alexander the Great*, Cambridge, 1988.

Cary, George, *The Medieval Alexander*, Cambridge, 1956.

Dawson, Doyne, *Cities of the Gods*, Oxford, 1992.

Friedman, John, *The Monstrous Races in Medieval Art and Thought*, Cambridge, Massachusetts, 1981.

Gunderson, Lloyd, *Alexander's Letter to Aristotle about India*, Meisenheim am Glan, 1980.

Halbfass, Wilhelm, *India and Europe*, Albany, 1988.

Harvey, P. D. A., *Medieval Maps*, London, 1991.

Karttunen, Klaus, *India in Early Greek Literature*, Helsinki, 1989.

Kazis, I. J., *The Gests of Alexander of Macedon*, Cambridge, Massachusetts, 1962.

Lascelles, Mary, 'Alexander and the Earthly Paradise in Medieval English Writings,' *Medium Aevum* 5 (1936), pp. 31–47, 79–104, 173–188.

Mandeville, John, *Mandeville's Travels*, edited by M. C. Seymour, Oxford, 1968.

Morgan, J. R. and Richard Stoneman, *Greek Fiction*, London, 1994.

Pfister, Friedrich, *Kleine Schriften zum Alexanderroman*, Meisenheim am Glan, 1975.

Phillips, J. R. S., *The Medieval Expansion of Europe*, Oxford, 1988.

Philostratus, *Life of Apollonius of Tyana*, translated by C. P. Jones, Harmondsworth, 1977.

Ross, D. J. A., *Alexander Historiatus: A Guide to Medieval Illustrated Alexander Literature*, London, 1963.

Stoneman, Richard (translator), *The Greek Alexander Romance*, Harmondsworth, 1991.

Stoneman, Richard, 'Romantic Ethnography: Central Asia and India in the Alexander Romance', *Ancient World*, 1994.

Stoneman, Richard, 'Who are the Brahmans?', *Classical Quarterly*, 1994.

Stoneman, Richard, 'Naked Philosophers', *Journal of Hellenic Studies* 75, 1995.
White, David Gordon, *Myths of the Dog-Man*, Chicago, 1991.

ANCIENT CLASSICS
IN EVERYMAN

A SELECTION

The Republic
PLATO
The most important and enduring of
Plato's works **£5.99**

The Education of Cyrus
XENOPHON
A fascinating insight into the culture
and politics of ancient Greece **£6.99**

Juvenal's Satires with the
Satires of Persius
JUVENAL AND PERSIUS
Unique and acute observations of
contemporary Roman society **£5.99**

The Odyssey
HOMER
A classic translation of one of the
greatest adventures ever told **£5.99**

History of the
Peloponnesian War
THUCYDIDES
The war that brought to an end a
golden age of democracy **£5.99**

The Histories
HERODOTUS
The earliest surviving work of
Greek prose literature **£7.99**

£5.99

AVAILABILITY

All books are available from your local bookshop or direct from
**Littlehampton Book Services Cash Sales, 14 Eldon Way, Lineside Estate,
Littlehampton, West Sussex BN17 7HE.** PRICES ARE SUBJECT TO CHANGE.

To order any of the books, please enclose a cheque (in £ sterling) made payable to
Littlehampton Book Services, or phone your order through with credit card details (Access,
Visa or Mastercard) on 0903 721596 (24 hour answering service) stating card number and
expiry date. Please add £1.25 for package and postage to the total value of your order.

In the USA, for further information and a complete catalogue call 1-800-526-2778.